Following a level path across the top of Hasty Bank

THE CLEVELAND WAY NATIONAL TRAIL

Officially opened in 1969, the Cleveland Way was the second national trail to be established in Britain. Stretching 110 miles (177km) from Helmsley to Filey, it takes in open heather moorlands, gentle dales and dramatic cliff coastline. The trail is suitable for walkers and trekkers at all levels of experience.

Contents and using this guide

This booklet of Ordnance Survey 1:25,000 Explorer maps has been designed for convenient use on the trail and includes:

- a key to map pages (page 2) showing where to find the maps for each stage
- the full and up-to-date line of the National Trail
- an extract from the OS Explorer map legend (pages 56–58)

In addition, the guidebook *Walking the Cleveland Way and Yorkshire Wolds Way* describes the full route with lots of other practical and historical information.

ISBN-13: 978 1 85284 934 4
Reprinted 2020 (with updates)

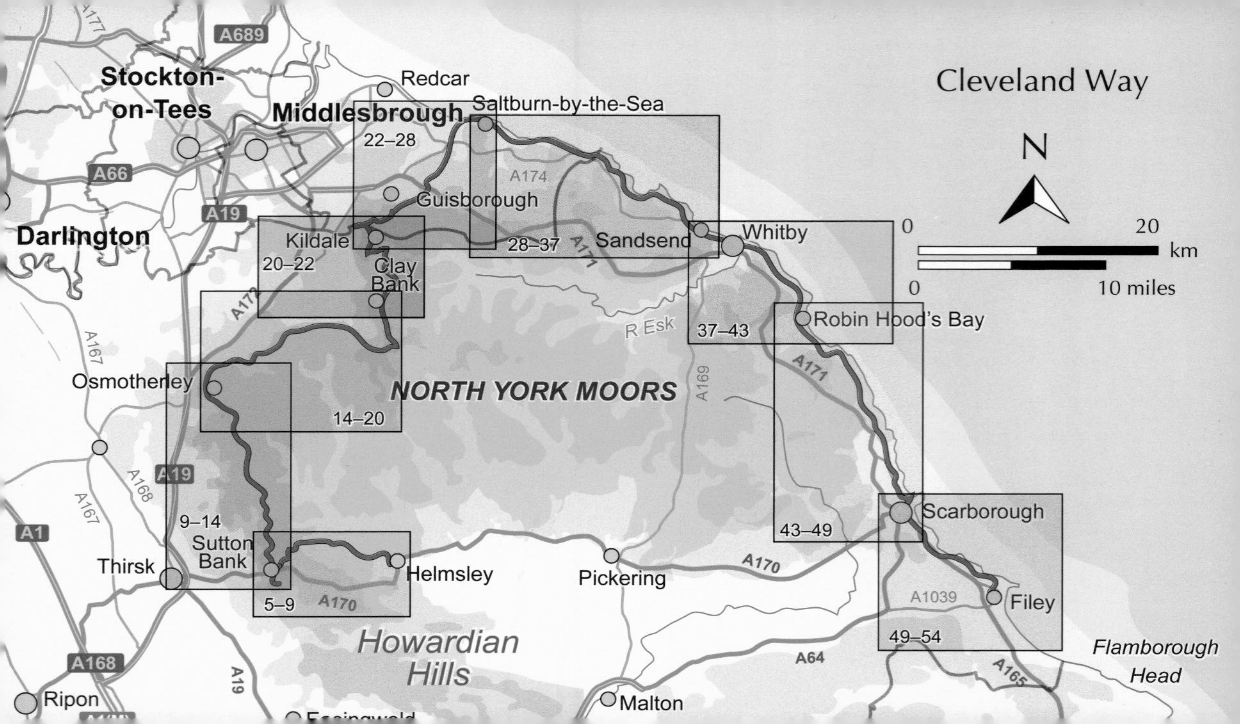

Cleveland Way
N
0
20
km
0
10 miles
Stockton-on-Tees
Middlesbrough
Redcar
Saltburn-by-the-Sea
Darlington
Guisborough
Kildale
Clay Bank
Whitby
Sandsend
Robin Hood's Bay
R Esk
NORTH YORK MOORS
Osmotherley
Sutton Bank
Thirsk
Helmsley
Pickering
Scarborough
Filey
Flamborough Head
Howardian Hills
Malton
Ripon
22–28
28–37
20–22
37–43
14–20
43–49
9–14
5–9
49–54
A689
A66
A19
A174
A171
A172
A169
A167
A168
A170
A1039
A64
A165
A1

THE CLEVELAND WAY NATIONAL TRAIL

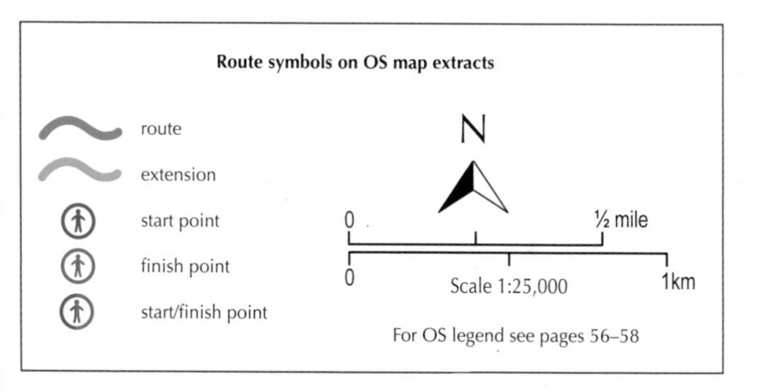

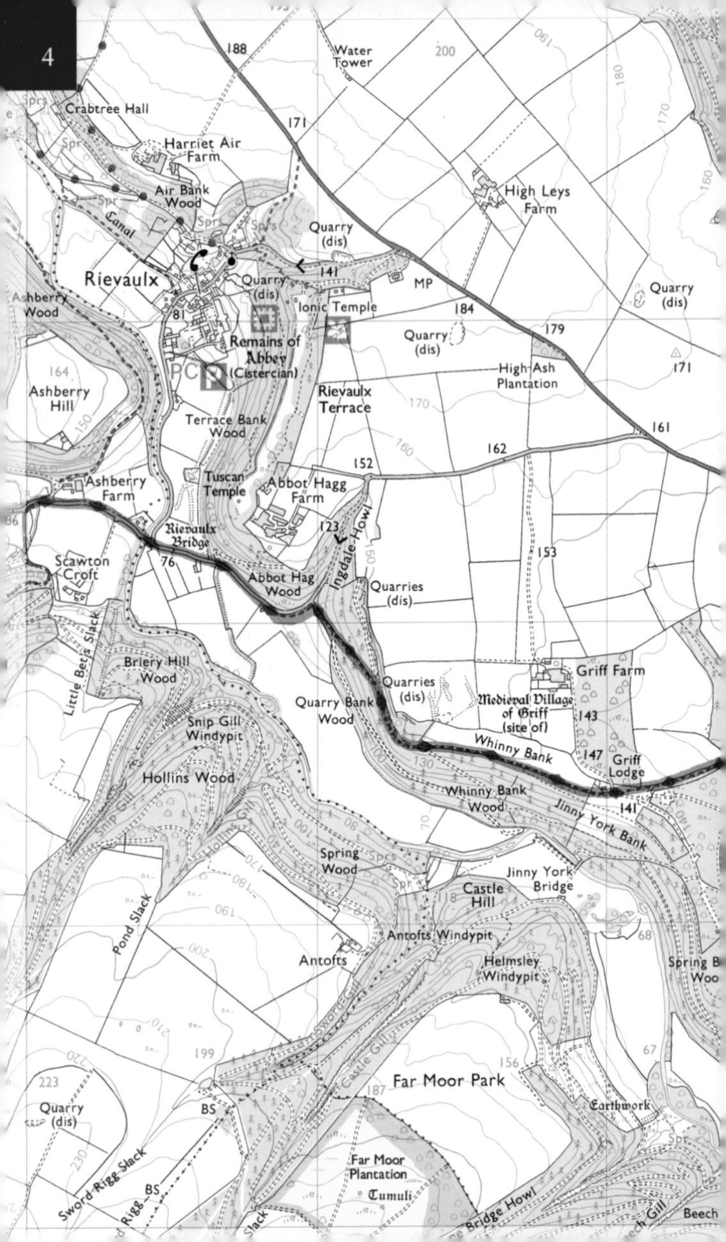
188
Water Tower
200
Crabtree Hall
Harriet Air Farm
171
Air Bank Wood
Canal
High Leys Farm
Quarry (dis)
Rievaulx
141
MP
Quarry (dis)
Ashberry Wood
81
Ionic Temple
184
Remains of Abbey (Cistercian)
Quarry (dis)
179
PC
High Ash Plantation
171
164
Ashberry Hill
Rievaulx Terrace
170
Terrace Bank Wood
161
162
152
Tuscan Temple
Abbot Hagg Farm
Ashberry Farm
123
Ingdale Howl
Rievaulx Bridge
153
Scawton Croft
76
Abbot Hag Wood
Quarries (dis)
Little Bet's Slack
Briery Hill Wood
Griff Farm
Quarries (dis)
Quarry Bank Wood
Medieval Village of Griff (site of)
143
Snip Gill Windypit
Whinny Bank
147
Griff Lodge
Hollins Wood
Whinny Bank Wood
141
Jinny York Bank
Snip Gill
Hollins Gill
Spring Wood
Jinny York Bridge
Castle Hill
118
Pond Slack
Antofts Windypit
68
Antofts
Helmsley Windypit
Sword Gill
199
223
Castle Gill
156
67
Far Moor Park
187
Quarry (dis)
BS
Earthwork
Sword Rigg Slack
Far Moor Plantation
Tumuli
BS
Bridge Howl
Beech

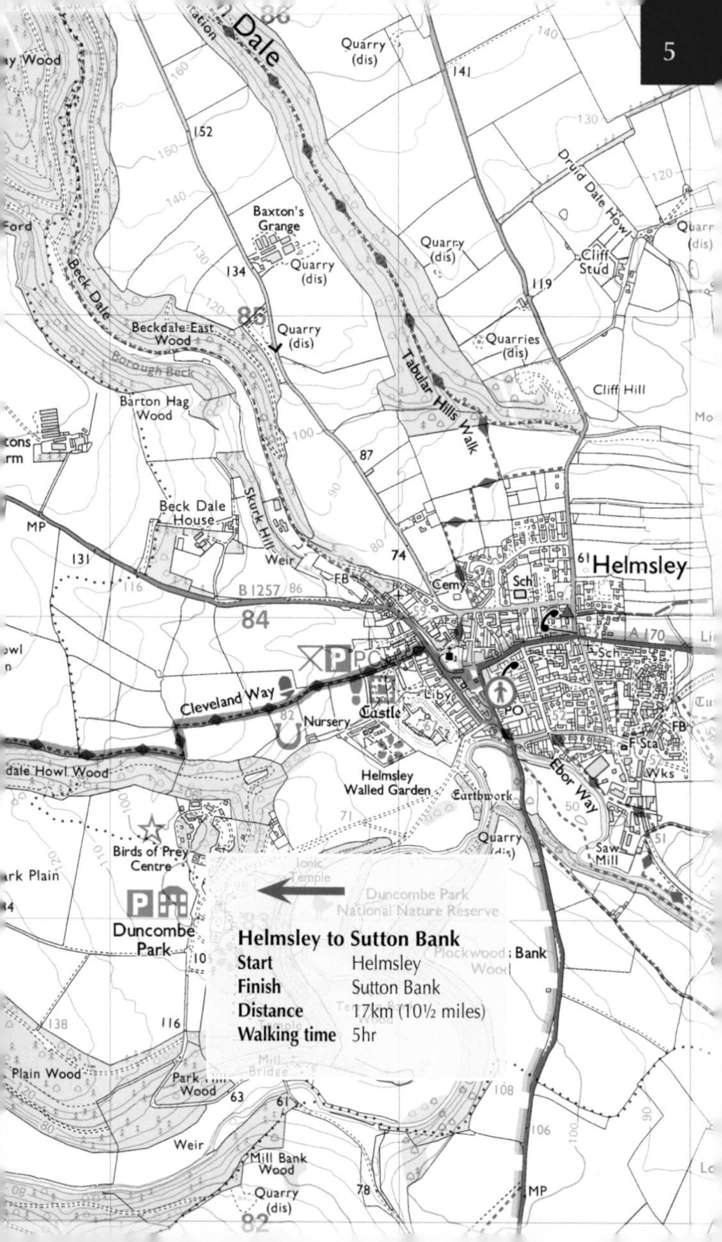

Helmsley to Sutton Bank

Start	Helmsley
Finish	Sutton Bank
Distance	17km (10½ miles)
Walking time	5hr

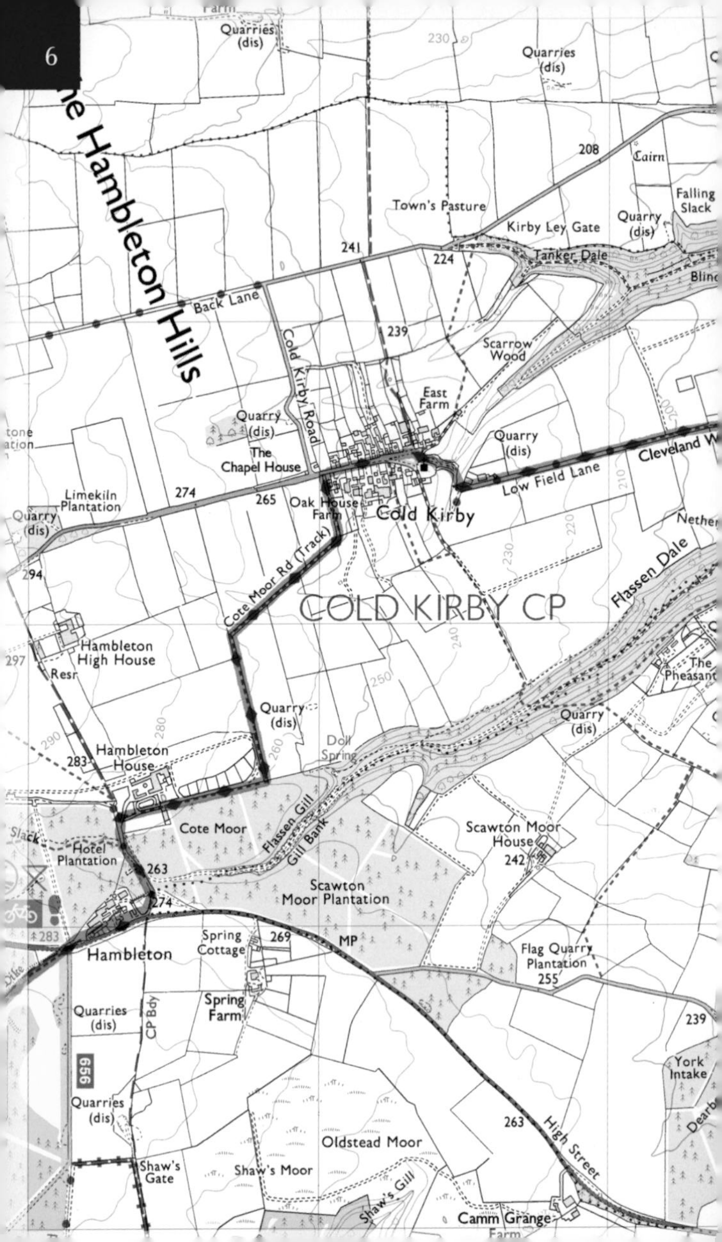

The Hambleton Hills
Quarries (dis)
Town's Pasture
Kirby Ley Gate
Tanker Dale
Cairn
Falling Slack
Quarry (dis)
Back Lane
Cold Kirby Road
Scarrow Wood
East Farm
The Chapel House
Low Field Lane
Cleveland Way
Limekiln Plantation
Oak House Farm
Cold Kirby
Cote Moor Rd (Track)
COLD KIRBY CP
Flassen Dale
Hambleton High House
Resr
The Pheasant
Doll Spring
Hambleton House
Cote Moor
Flassen Gill
Gill Bank
Scawton Moor House
Hotel Plantation
Scawton Moor Plantation
Spring Cottage
MP
Hambleton
Flag Quarry Plantation
Spring Farm
CP Bdy
York Intake
Oldstead Moor
High Street
Shaw's Gate
Shaw's Moor
Shaw's Gill
Camm Grange Farm

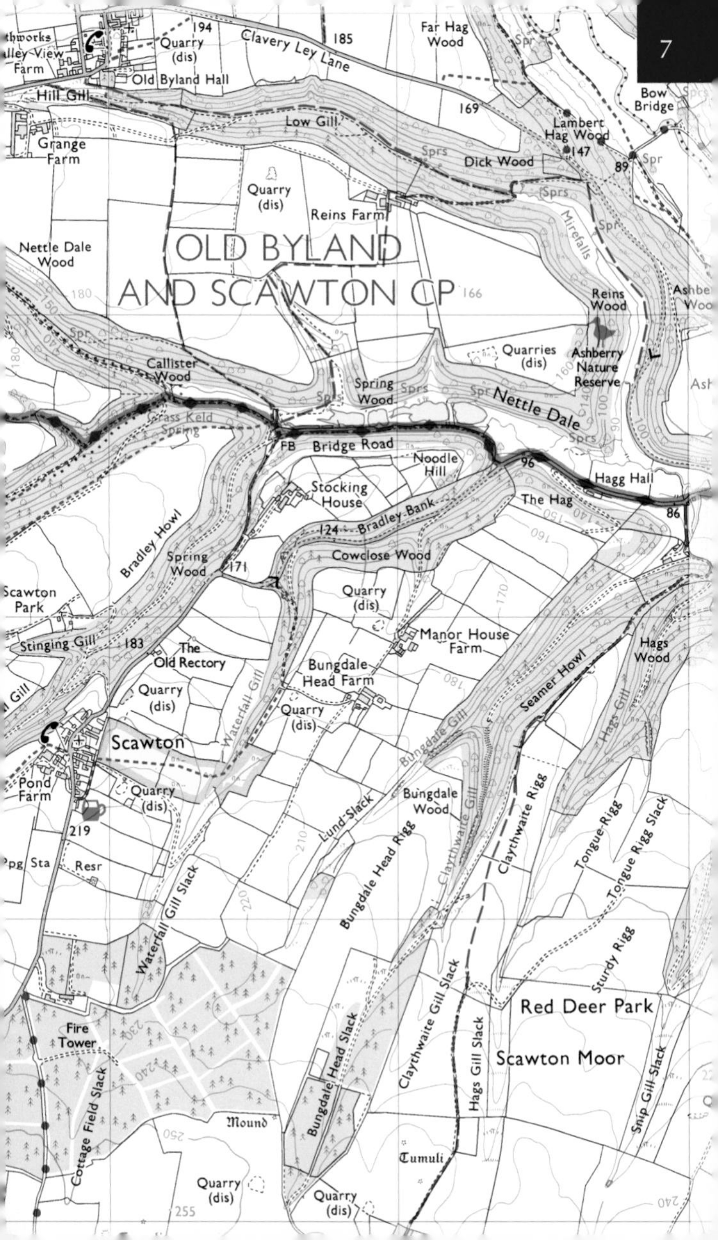

OLD BYLAND AND SCAWTON CP
Old Byland Hall
Valley View Farm
Quarry (dis)
Clavery Ley Lane
Far Hag Wood
Hill Gill
Low Gill
Grange Farm
Bow Bridge
Lambert Hag Wood
Dick Wood
Reins Farm
Mirefalls
Nettle Dale Wood
Reins Wood
Ashberry Nature Reserve
Quarries (dis)
Callister Wood
Spring Wood
Nettle Dale
Grass Keld Spring
FB
Bridge Road
Noodle Hill
Hagg Hall
The Hag
Stocking House
Bradley Bank
Cowclose Wood
Bradley Howl
Spring Wood
Scawton Park
Stinging Gill
The Old Rectory
Manor House Farm
Bungdale Head Farm
Hags Wood
Seamer Howl
Hags Gill
Waterfall Gill
Bungdale Gill
Scawton
Pond Farm
Bungdale Wood
Claythwaite Gill
Claythwaite Rigg
Tongue Rigg
Tongue Rigg Slack
Lund Slack
Bungdale Head Rigg
Ppg Sta
Resr
Waterfall Gill Slack
Sturdy Rigg
Red Deer Park
Scawton Moor
Fire Tower
Claythwaite Gill Slack
Hags Gill Slack
Bungdale Head Slack
Snip Gill Slack
Cottage Field Slack
Mound
Tumuli

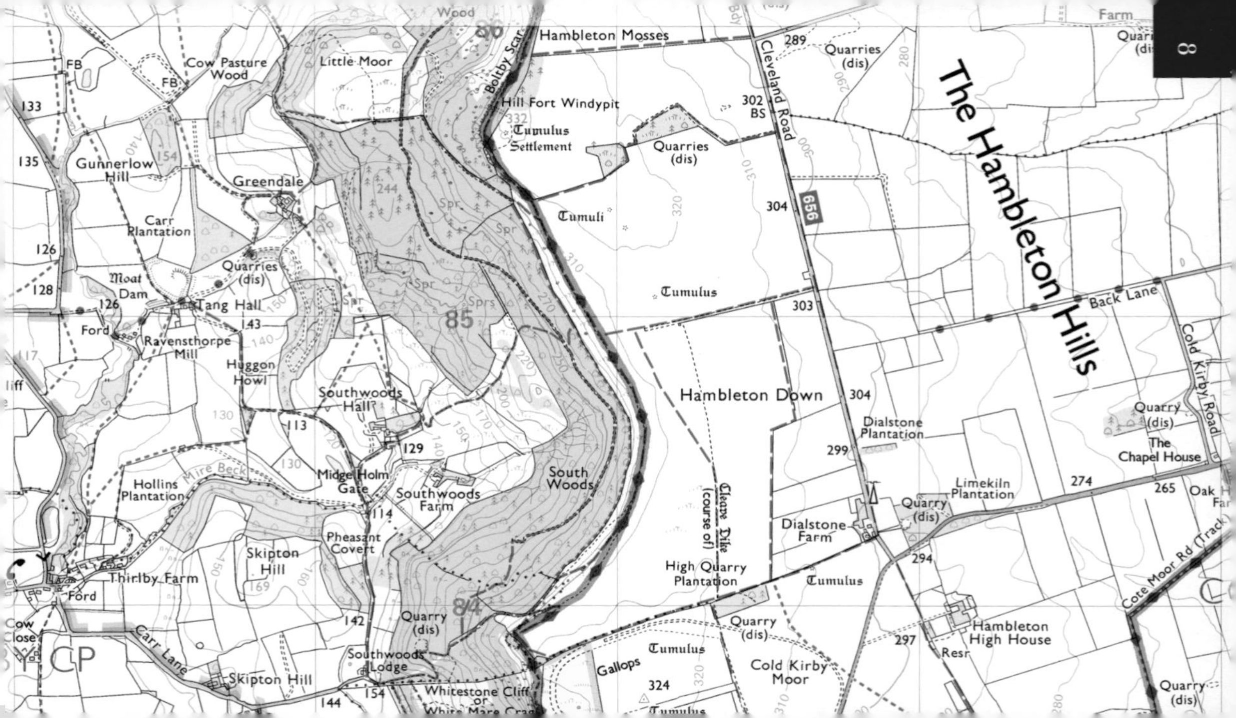
The Hambleton Hills
Hambleton Mosses
Little Moor
Cow Pasture Wood
FB
FB
133
135
Gunnerlow Hill
154
Greendale
244
Carr Plantation
126
Moat
Dam
128
126
Quarries (dis)
Tang Hall
143
Ford
Ravensthorpe Mill
Huggon Howl
Southwoods Hall
113
129
130
Hollins Plantation
Mire Beck
Midge Holm Gate
Southwoods Farm
114
South Woods
Pheasant Covert
Skipton Hill
169
Thirlby Farm
Ford
Cow Close
CP
Carr Lane
Skipton Hill
142
Quarry (dis)
Southwoods Lodge
144
154
Whitestone Cliff or White Mare Crag
85
84
Spr
Sprs
Boltby Scar
Hill Fort Windypit
332
Tumulus
Settlement
Quarries (dis)
Tumuli
Tumulus
Wood
Farm
289
Quarries (dis)
Cleveland Road
302
BS
304
656
303
Back Lane
Hambleton Down
304
Cleave Dike
(course of)
High Quarry Plantation
Tumulus
Quarry (dis)
Gallops
Tumulus
324
Cold Kirby Moor
Dialstone Plantation
299
Dialstone Farm
Quarry (dis)
Limekiln Plantation
274
265
Oak
294
297
Resr
Hambleton High House
Cote Moor Rd (Track)
Quarry (dis)
Cold Kirby Road
Quarry (dis)
The Chapel House

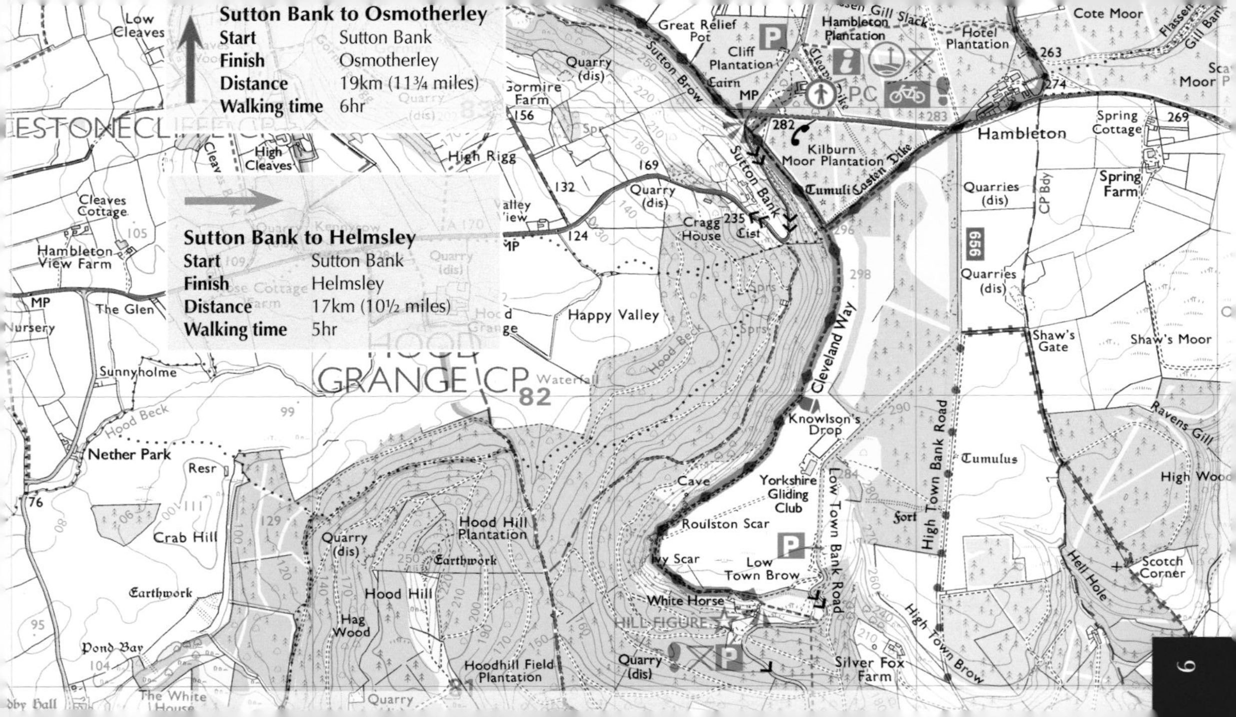

Sutton Bank to Osmotherley
Start Sutton Bank
Finish Osmotherley
Distance 19km (11¾ miles)
Walking time 6hr
Sutton Bank to Helmsley
Start Sutton Bank
Finish Helmsley
Distance 17km (10½ miles)
Walking time 5hr
Low Cleaves
High Cleaves
Cleaves Cottage
Hambleton View Farm
The Glen
Nursery
Sunnyholme
Hood Beck
Nether Park
Resr
Crab Hill
Earthwork
Pond Bay
The White House
HOOD GRANGE CP
Waterfall
Gormire Farm
High Rigg
Valley View
Happy Valley
Quarry (dis)
Cragg House
Cist
Sutton Brow
Great Relief Pot
Cliff Plantation
Cairn
Sutton Bank
Hambleton Plantation
Hotel Plantation
Kilburn Moor Plantation
Casten Dike
Tumuli
Hambleton
Cote Moor
Spring Cottage
Spring Farm
Quarries (dis)
CP Bdy
Shaw's Gate
Shaw's Moor
Cleveland Way
Knowlson's Drop
Yorkshire Gliding Club
Cave
Roulston Scar
Ivy Scar
Low Town Brow
Low Town Bank Road
White Horse
HILL FIGURE
Hood Hill Plantation
Hood Hill
Hag Wood
Hoodhill Field Plantation
High Town Bank Road
Tumulus
Fort
High Town Brow
Silver Fox Farm
Ravens Gill
High Wood
Hell Hole
Scotch Corner

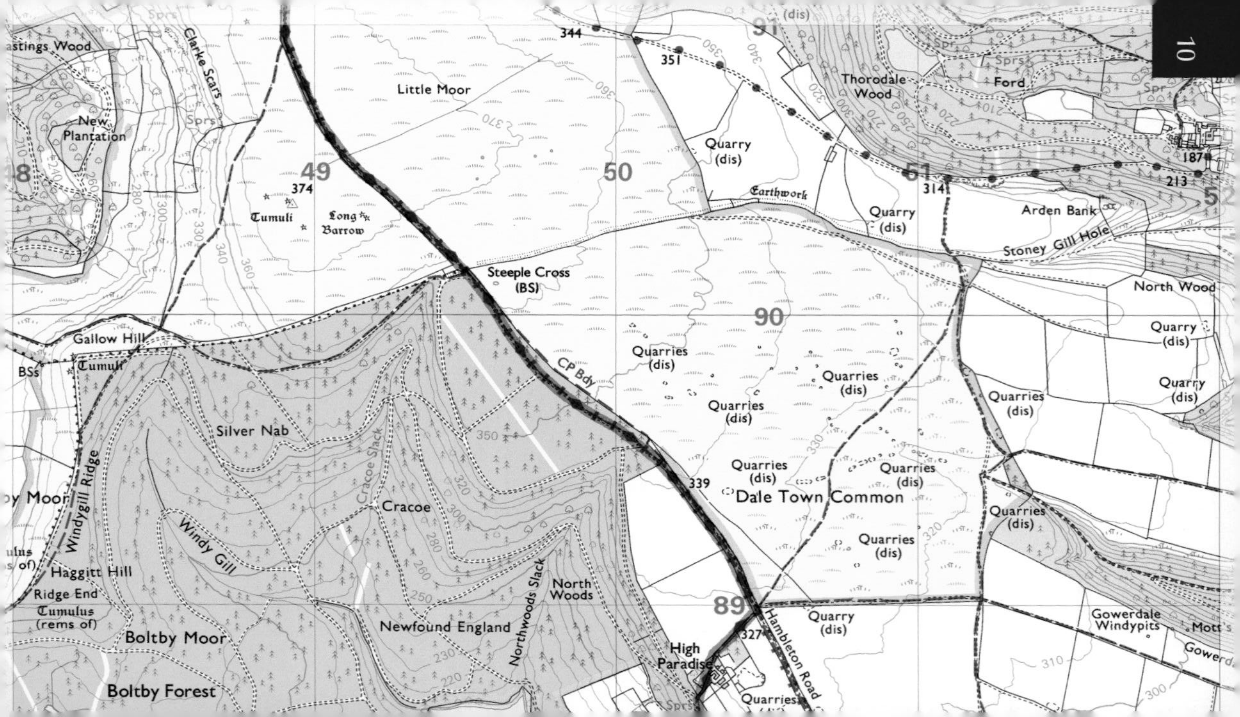

Thorodale Wood
Ford
Arden Bank
Stoney Gill Hole
North Wood
Quarry (dis)
Quarries (dis)
Earthwork
Dale Town Common
Hambleton Road
High Paradise
Gowerdale Windypits
Mott's
Steeple Cross (BS)
CP Bdy
Little Moor
Long Barrow
Tumuli
Clarke Scars
New Plantation
Gallow Hill
Silver Nab
Windy Gill
Cracoe
Cracoe Slack
North Woods
Northwoods Slack
Newfound England
Boltby Moor
Boltby Forest
Haggitt Hill
Windygill Ridge
Ridge End
Tumulus (rems of)
Spr
Sprs
344
351
374
339
327
314
213
187

Bleaky Hill
269
Low Paradise Farm
Low Paradise Wood
Moor Ings
310
Tumulus
Silver Hill Farm
303
Quarry (dis)
Tumulus
Tumulus
311
88
Gurtof Wood
260
250
240
210
200
190
170
306
Hesketh Dike
Sneck Yate
Silver Hill Tumulus
Sneck Yate Plantation
Hell Hole
Quarry (dis)
Moor
Bower Bank
249
Lunshaw House
BOLTBY CP
Spring Wood
239
Sneck Yate Bank
Cleveland Way
299
Sled Hill
Spr
Sprs
Lunshaw Beck
Thicket Wood
188
Low Wood
280
300
290
296
Quarry (dis)
Thwaite Stones
Water Works
Hesketh Hall
149
Hesketh Grange
87
298
Quarry (dis)
King Spring
Ravensthorpe Manor
Boltby
153
Quarries (dis)
155
141
Tumulus
313
High Barn
Long Plain Farm
West Gurtof Farm
146
Tumulus
310
166
140
Holme Hole
Tumulus
295
Limperdale
Town Pasture Farm
137
Ford
FB
Tips (dis)
Quarry (dis)
289
Quarries (dis)
West Acre Lodge
136
Gurtof Beck
Quarry (dis)
174
Quarries (dis)
138
Town's Pasture Wood
CP Bdy
Quarry (dis)
Hales
Hambleton Mosses
289

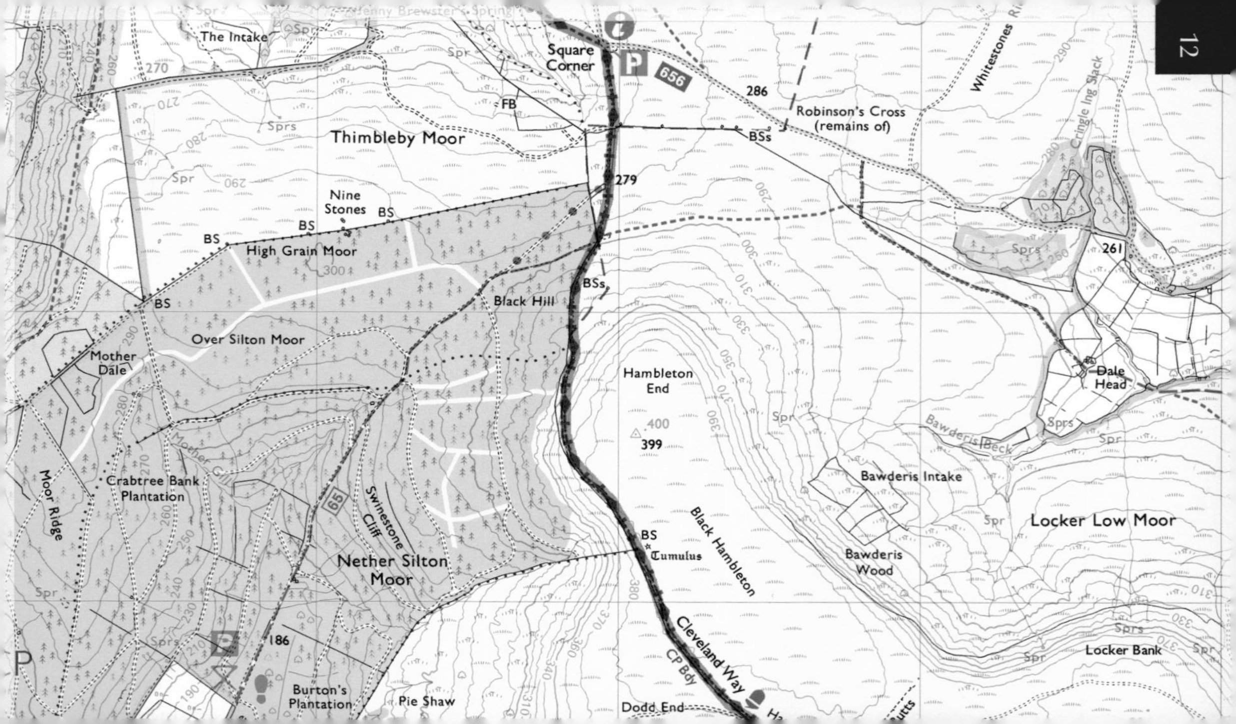

Jenny Brewster's Spring
The Intake
Square Corner
656
286
Whitestones
Robinson's Cross
(remains of)
Cringle Ing Slack
FB
Thimbleby Moor
BSs
279
Nine Stones
BS
High Grain Moor
261
Black Hill
Over Silton Moor
Mother Dale
Hambleton End
Dale Head
399
Bawderis Beck
Moor Ridge
Crabtree Bank Plantation
65
Swinestone Cliff
Bawderis Intake
Locker Low Moor
Tumulus
Black Hambleton
Nether Silton Moor
Bawderis Wood
Cleveland Way
CP Bdy
186
Locker Bank
Burton's Plantation
Pie Shaw
Dodd End

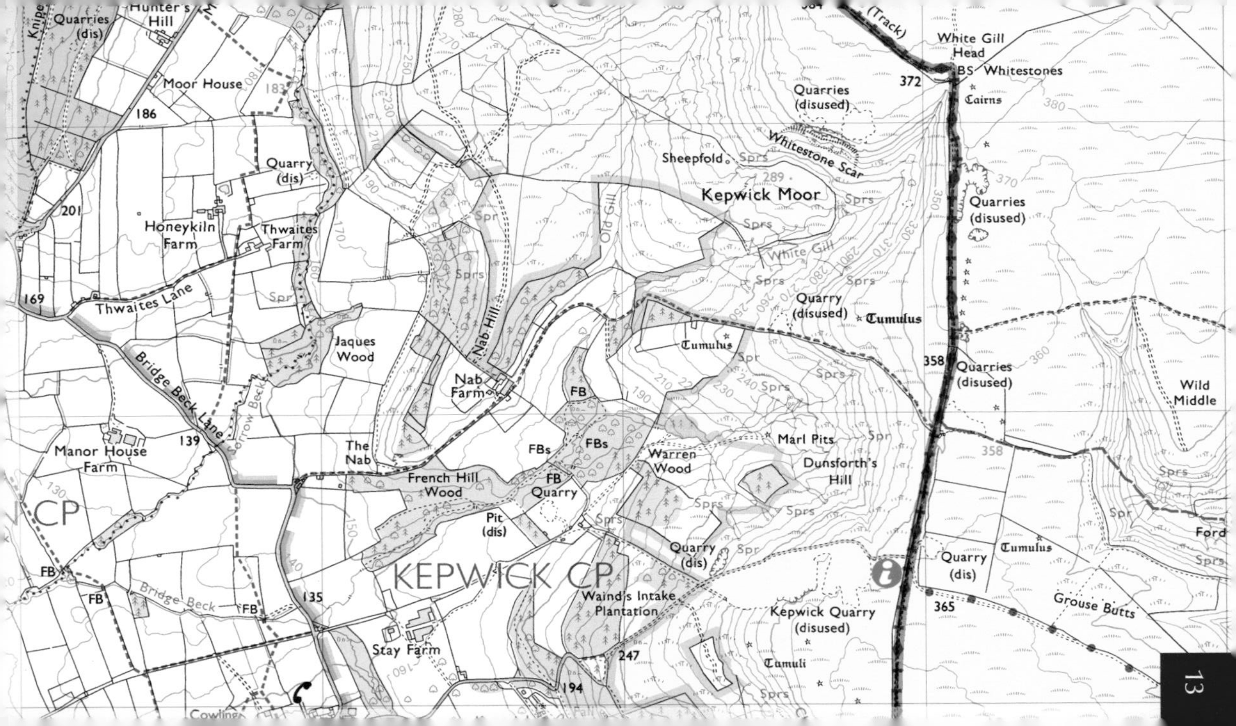
Knipe
Quarries (dis)
Hunter's Hill
Moor House
186
201
169
Honeykiln Farm
Thwaites Farm
Quarry (dis)
Thwaites Lane
Jaques Wood
Bridge Beck Lane
139
Manor House Farm
CP
FB
Bridge Beck
135
Stay Farm
Cowlings
The Nab
French Hill Wood
Pit (dis)
FBs
FB
Quarry
Nab Hill
Nab Farm
Old Gill
Sheepfold
Kepwick Moor
289
Whitestone Scar
Quarries (disused)
White Gill
Quarry (disused)
Tumulus
Marl Pits
Warren Wood
Dunsforth's Hill
Quarry (dis)
KEPWICK CP
Waind's Intake Plantation
247
194
Kepwick Quarry (disused)
Tumuli
(Track)
White Gill Head
BS Whitestones
372
Cairns
358
Quarries (disused)
Wild Middle
Ford
Tumulus
Quarry (dis)
365
Grouse Butts

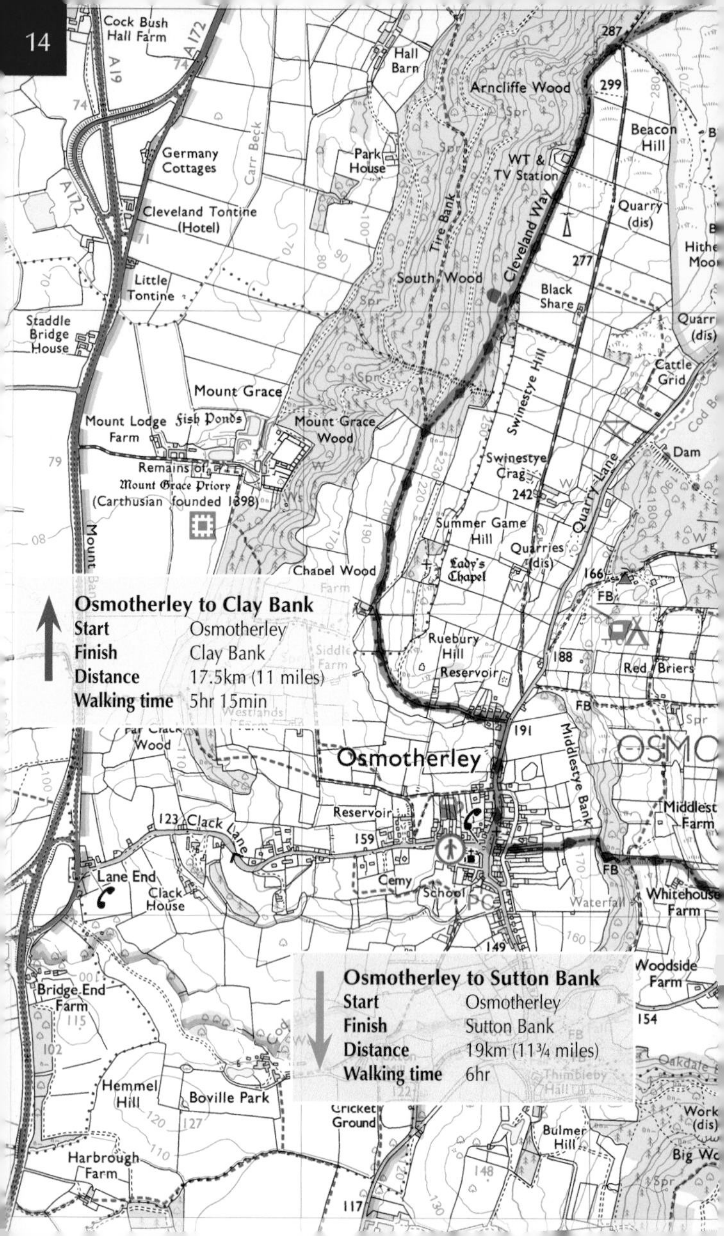
Cock Bush Hall Farm
A172
A19
Hall Barn
Arncliffe Wood
287
299
Beacon Hill
Germany Cottages
Carr Beck
Park House
WT & TV Station
Cleveland Way
Quarry (dis)
Cleveland Tontine (Hotel)
Tire Bank
Little Tontine
South Wood
277
Black Share
Staddle Bridge House
Quarry (dis)
Swinestye Hill
Cattle Grid
Mount Grace
Mount Lodge Farm
Fish Ponds
Mount Grace Wood
Dam
Remains of
Mount Grace Priory
(Carthusian founded 1398)
Swinestye Crag
242
Quarry Lane
Summer Game Hill
Quarries (dis)
Lady's Chapel
Chapel Wood
166
FB
Osmotherley to Clay Bank
Start Osmotherley
Finish Clay Bank
Distance 17.5km (11 miles)
Walking time 5hr 15min
Ruebury Hill
Reservoir
188
Red Briers
Wood
191
Middlestye Bank
Osmotherley
Reservoir
123 Clack Lane
159
Middlest Farm
Lane End
Clack House
Cemy
School
PC
Waterfall
Whitehouse Farm
149
Woodside Farm
Osmotherley to Sutton Bank
Start Osmotherley
Finish Sutton Bank
Distance 19km (11¾ miles)
Walking time 6hr
Bridge End Farm
154
Hemmel Hill
Boville Park
Cricket Ground
Bulmer Hill
Harbrough Farm
Big Wo
148
117

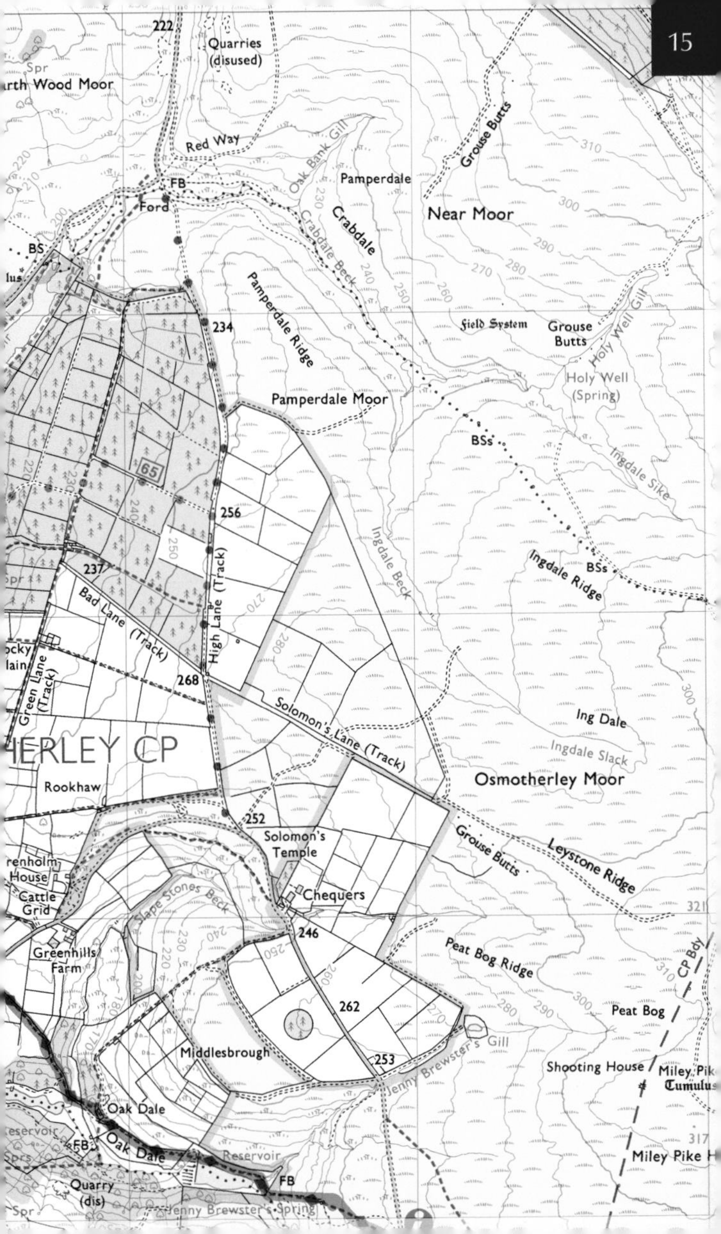
222
Quarries
(disused)
Spr
Wood Moor
Red Way
Oak Bank Gill
Grouse Butts
310
FB
Ford
Pamperdale
300
Near Moor
Crabdale
Crabdale Beck
290
280
270
BS
Pamperdale Ridge
234
Field System
Grouse
Butts
Holy Well Gill
Holy Well
(Spring)
Pamperdale Moor
BSs
Ingdale Sike
65
256
Ingdale Beck
Ingdale Ridge
BSs
237
Bad Lane (Track)
High Lane (Track)
Green Lane
(Track)
268
Solomon's Lane (Track)
300
Ing Dale
Ingdale Slack
HERLEY CP
Osmotherley Moor
Rookhaw
252
Solomon's
Temple
Grouse Butts
Leystone Ridge
House
Cattle
Grid
Chequers
Slape Stones Beck
246
321
Peat Bog Ridge
CP Bdy
Greenhills
Farm
262
Peat Bog
Jenny Brewster's Gill
Middlesbrough
253
Shooting House
Miley Pike
Tumulus
Oak Dale
Oak Dale
317
FB
Reservoir
Miley Pike
Quarry
(dis)
FB
Jenny Brewster's Spring
Spr

Thorn Hill
Gold Hill
Goldgate Bridge
Woodbine House
Ford
Castle (rems of)
Church (rems of)
MS
Toft Hill
West Lees
Swainby
PC
Foot Bridge
Howe Hill
Sch
Beck Close Hill
Scarth Wood Farm
Back Lane
Mill Farm
Carr Beck
Billimore Hill
Shepherd Hill
Ford
Scarth Lees
Scarth Nick Farm
FB
Dismtd Rly
Coalmire Lane
Scarth Wood Farm
Ford
Round Hill
Spr
Scarth Wood
Sprs
Clain Wood
Cattle Grid
Coalmire
Limek Bank
Tumuli
Whorlton Moor
Raindrip Well
Quarries (disused)
Scarth Wood Moor
Spr
Beacon Hill
BS
Red Way
Oak Bank Gill
Grouse Butts
Pamperdale
Quarry (dis)
FB
Ford
Crabdale
Crabdale Beck
Near Moor
Hither Moor
Tumulus
Pamperdal
Quarries

Whorl Hill Farm
Low Farm
126
Whorl Hill Wood
237
Whorl Hill
High Farm
Whorlton
Tips (dis)
Bank Lane
Faceby Beck
Mere Beck
Bracken Hill
122
Whorlton Lane
Whorlton House
Madewell Hill
02
Little Bonny Cliff
141
Faceby Plantation
Spr
Perish Crook
BS
Gold Hill
Knolls End
BSs
Cairn
Field System
Round Hill
Live Moor
01
Harpley's Well
Heathwaite
Live Moor Plantation
Air Shaft (dis)
Sprs
139
Huthwaite Green
Scugdale
Hollin Hill
Sunny Side
Fog Close
49
Weir
Scugdale Beck
50
Ford
Swine Park
165
Sparrow Hall
186
Snotterdale
Pit (dis)
Round Hill
WHORLTON CP
Harfa House
00
Tip (dis)
176
Harfa Bank Farm
Tips (disused)
Capper's Intake
Cow Kill Nab
Tips (disused)
Grouse Butts
Pin Howe
Piper Grain
Far Moor
Coal Hill
99
Stony

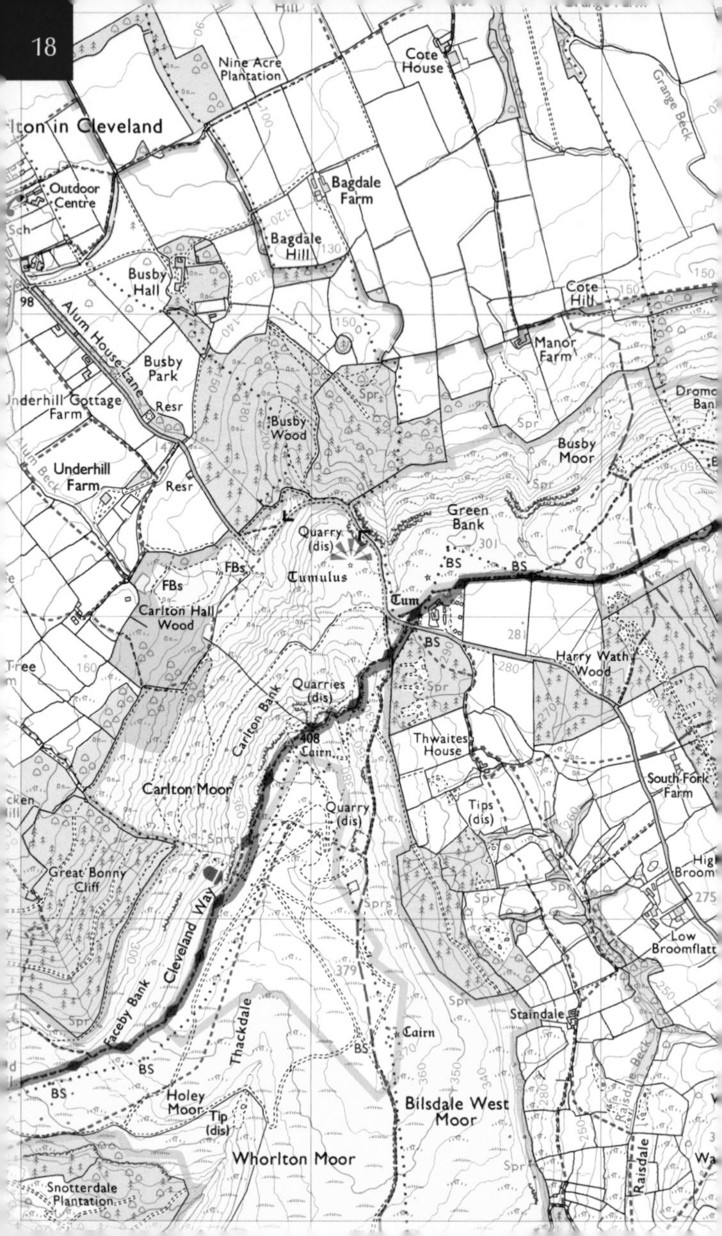

Nine Acre Plantation
Cote House
Grange Beck
Outdoor Centre
Sch
Bagdale Farm
Bagdale Hill
Busby Hall
Alum House Lane
Busby Park
Underhill Cottage Farm
Resr
Busby Wood
Cote Hill
Manor Farm
Busby Moor
Spr
Underhill Farm
Alum Beck
Green Bank
Quarry (dis)
Tumulus
BS
Tum
FBs
Carlton Hall Wood
Harry Wath Wood
Quarries (dis)
Carlton Bank
408
Cairn
Thwaites House
South Fork Farm
Carlton Moor
Quarry (dis)
Tips (dis)
Great Bonny Cliff
Sprs
Cleveland Way
Faceby Bank
Thackdale
379
Cairn
Staindale
Low Broomflatt
Raisdale Beck
Holey Moor
Tip (dis)
Bilsdale West Moor
Whorlton Moor
Snotterdale Plantation
Raisdale

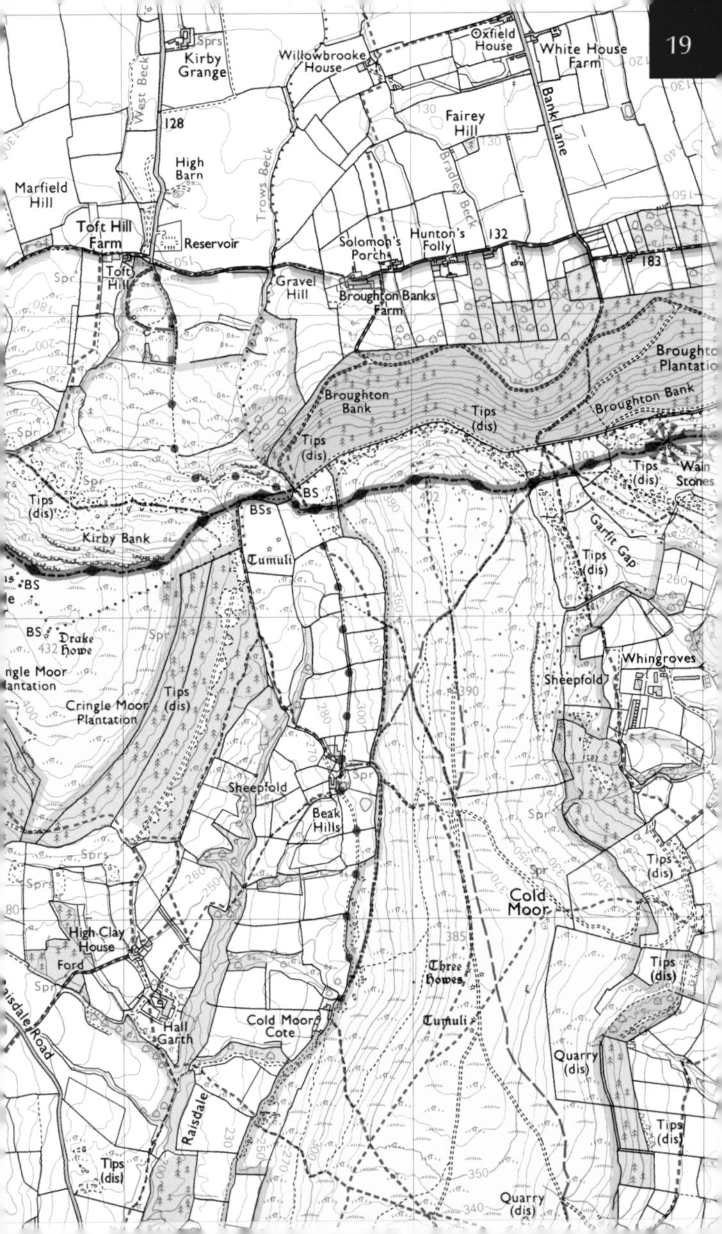
Kirby Grange
West Beck
Willowbrooke House
Oxfield House
White House Farm
Bank Lane
Fairey Hill
Bradley Beck
High Barn
Marfield Hill
Trows Beck
Toft Hill Farm
Reservoir
Solomon's Porch
Hunton's Folly
Toft Hill
Gravel Hill
Broughton Banks Farm
Broughton Plantation
Broughton Bank
Tips (dis)
Wain Stones
Kirby Bank
BS
BSs
Tumuli
Garfit Gap
Drake Howe
Cringle Moor Plantation
Whingroves
Sheepfold
Beak Hills
Cold Moor
High Clay House
Ford
Hall Garth
Cold Moor Cote
Three Howes
Quarry (dis)
Raisdale
Raisdale Road

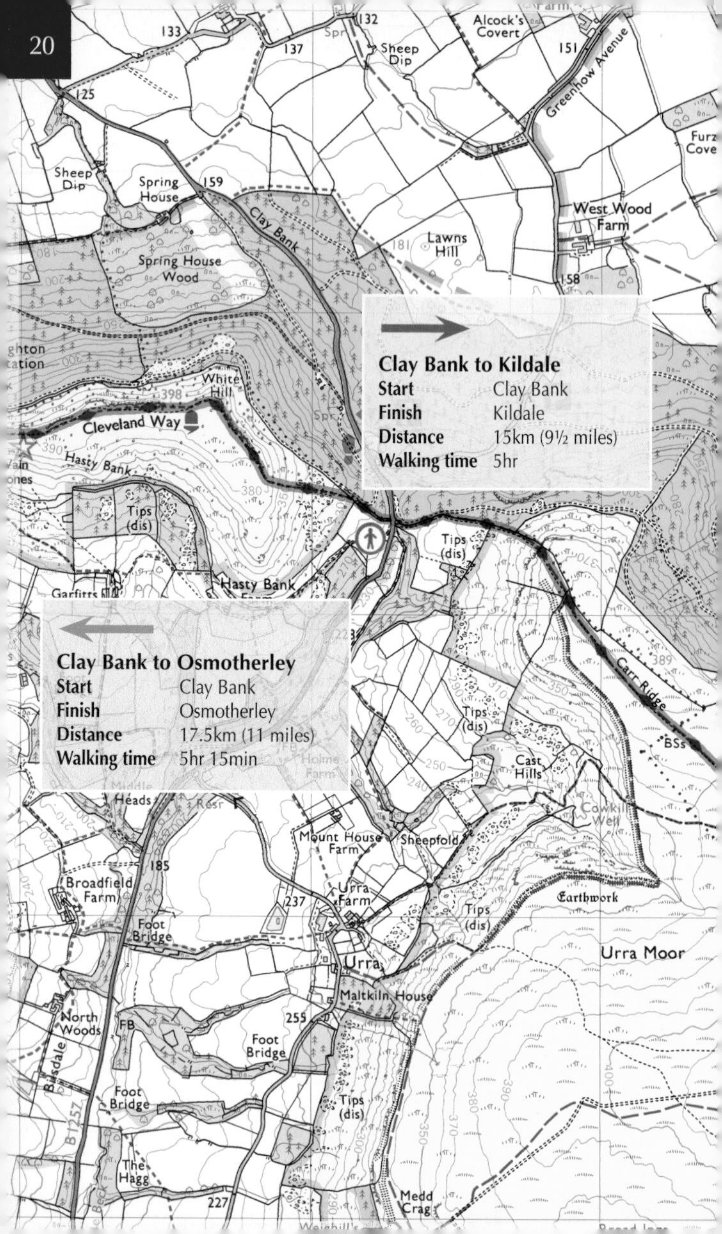
Clay Bank to Kildale
Start Clay Bank
Finish Kildale
Distance 15km (9½ miles)
Walking time 5hr
Clay Bank to Osmotherley
Start Clay Bank
Finish Osmotherley
Distance 17.5km (11 miles)
Walking time 5hr 15min
Cleveland Way
Clay Bank
Spring House Wood
Spring House
Sheep Dip
Alcock's Covert
Greenhow Avenue
West Wood Farm
Lawns Hill
White Hill
Hasty Bank
Hasty Bank Farm
Tips (dis)
Carr Ridge
Cast Hills
Cowkill Well
Earthwork
Urra Moor
Mount House Farm
Sheepfold
Urra Farm
Urra
Maltkiln House
Broadfield Farm
Foot Bridge
North Woods
Bilsdale
B1257
The Hagg
Medd Crag
Middle Heads

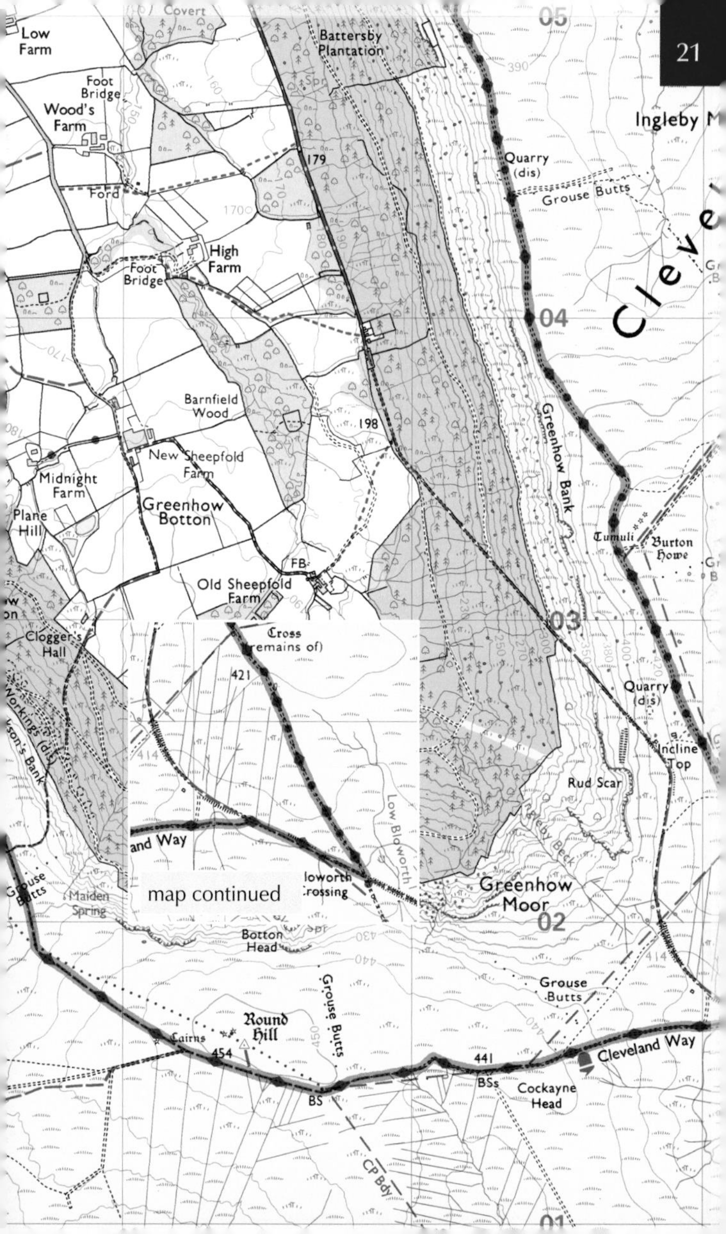
Low Farm
Covert
Battersby Plantation
Foot Bridge
Wood's Farm
Ingleby
Quarry (dis)
Grouse Butts
Ford
High Farm
Foot Bridge
Cleve
Barnfield Wood
Greenhow Bank
New Sheepfold Farm
Midnight Farm
Greenhow Botton
Plane Hill
Tumuli
Burton Howe
FB
Old Sheepfold Farm
Clogger's Hall
Cross (remains of)
Quarry (dis)
Incline Top
Rud Scar
and Way
Low Blowarth
Ingleby Beck
Greenhow Moor
Grouse Butts
Maiden Spring
map continued
Botton Head
Grouse Butts
Grouse Butts
Round Hill
Cairns
Cleveland Way
BS
BSs
Cockayne Head
CP Bdy

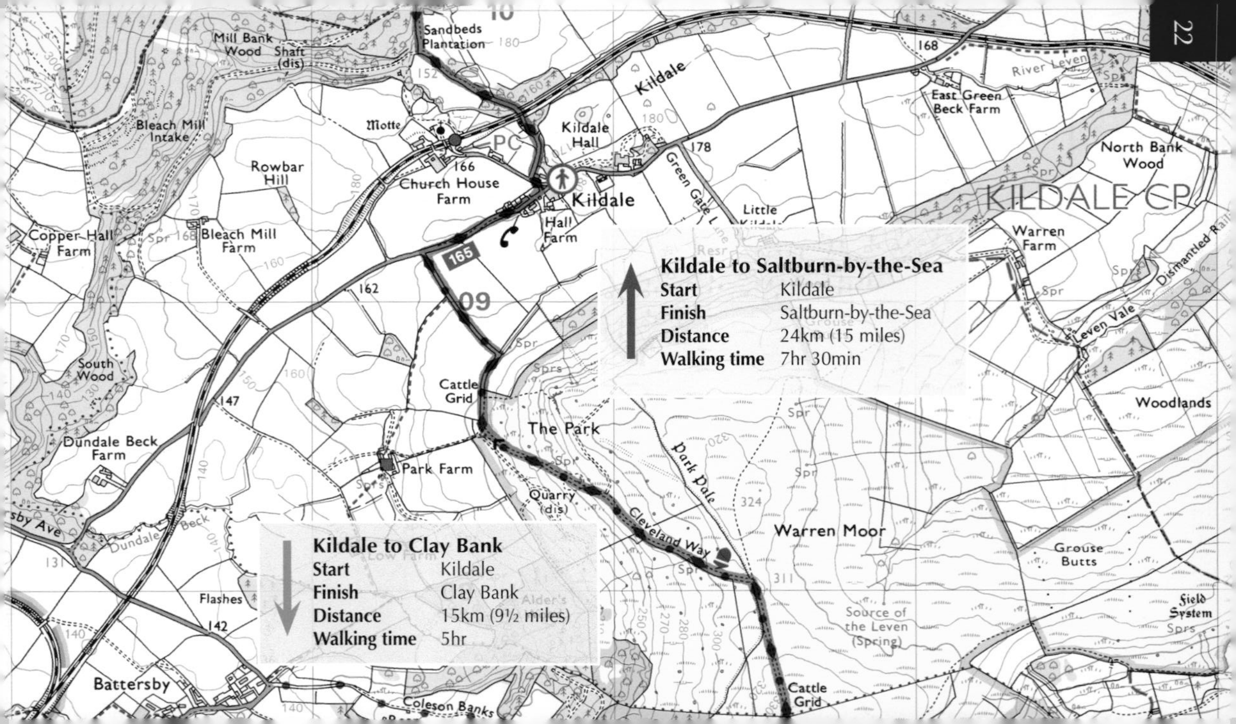
Kildale to Saltburn-by-the-Sea
Start Kildale
Finish Saltburn-by-the-Sea
Distance 24km (15 miles)
Walking time 7hr 30min
Kildale to Clay Bank
Start Kildale
Finish Clay Bank
Distance 15km (9½ miles)
Walking time 5hr
Sandbeds Plantation
Mill Bank Wood
Shaft (dis)
Bleach Mill Intake
Motte
PC
Church House Farm
Rowbar Hill
Kildale Hall
Kildale
Green Gate Lane
Little
Hall Farm
Copper Hall Farm
Bleach Mill Farm
165
09
162
South Wood
Cattle Grid
The Park
147
Dundale Beck Farm
Park Farm
Quarry (dis)
Cleveland Way
Park Pale
324
Warren Moor
311
Source of the Leven (Spring)
Cattle Grid
Flashes
142
Battersby
Coleson Banks
Dundale Beck
168
River Leven
East Green Beck Farm
178
North Bank Wood
KILDALE CP
Warren Farm
Dismantled Rail
Leven Vale
Woodlands
Grouse Butts
Field System

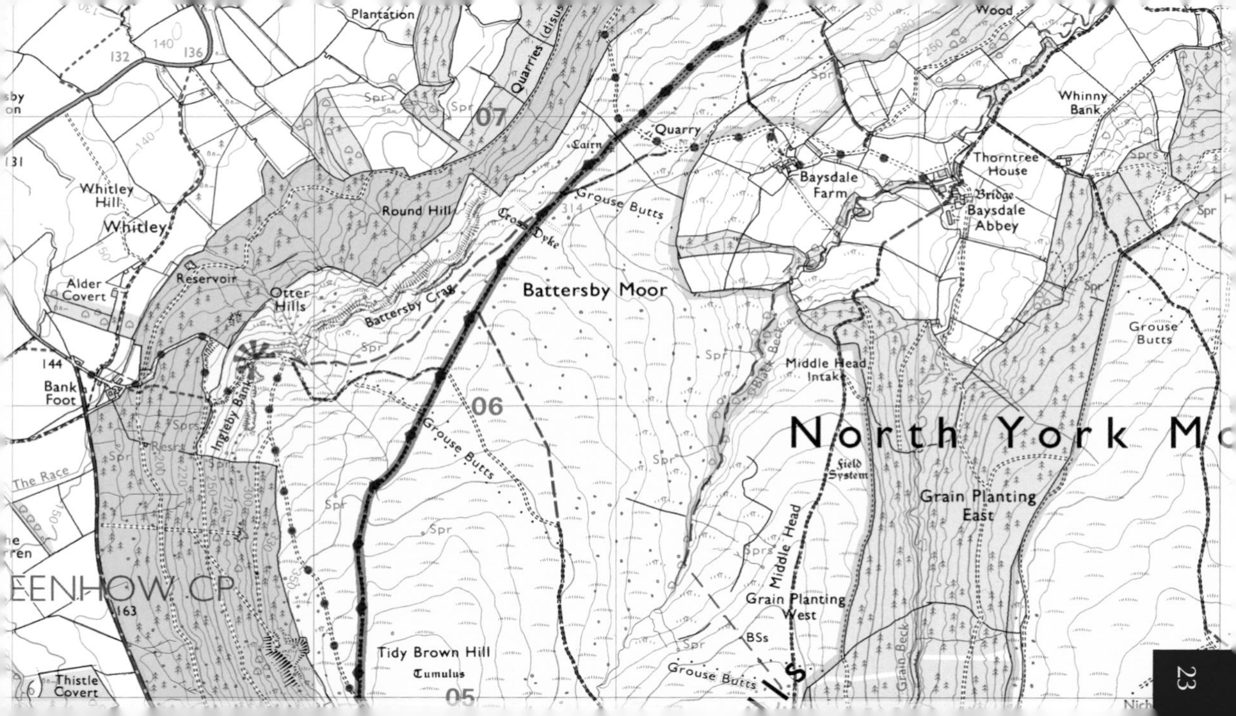

Plantation
Wood
Quarries (disus
07
Whinny Bank
Quarry
Cairn
Thorntree House
Baysdale Farm
Bridge
Baysdale Abbey
Whitley Hill
Whitley
Round Hill
Grouse Butts
314
Cross Dyke
Alder Covert
Reservoir
Otter Hills
Battersby Crag
Battersby Moor
Grouse Butts
144
Bank Foot
Ingleby Bank
Middle Head Intake
Black Beck
06
Grouse Butts
North York Mo
Field System
Grain Planting East
The Race
Resr
Middle Head
EENHOW CP
163
Grain Planting West
BSs
Tidy Brown Hill
Tumulus
Grouse Butts
Grain Beck
Thistle Covert
05

Pinchinthorpe House
Ward's Belt
High Farm
Pinchinthorpe Hall
Green Hills
Hall Hill
Newton under Roseberry
Rye Banks
Roseberry Lane
P
PC
Bousdale Farm
Bousdale Hill
Bousdale Wood
High Bousdale Wood
Mount House Farm
Brant Gate (Path)
Roseberry Common
Roseberry Well
Cleveland Way
Cairns
Newton Moor
Hutton Gate
Home Farm
Hutton Hall
Hutton Lowcross Woods
Hanging Stone
Hanging Stone Wood
Blue Lake Wood
Air Shaft (disused)
Hutton Wood
Hutton Moor
Black Nab
The Race
Sprs
Codhill Slack
Schs
Reed's Wood
Hill Plain
Cairn
Kemplah Wood
Tees Link
Hutton Village
Shaft (dis)
Bold Venture Gill
Highcliffe Farm

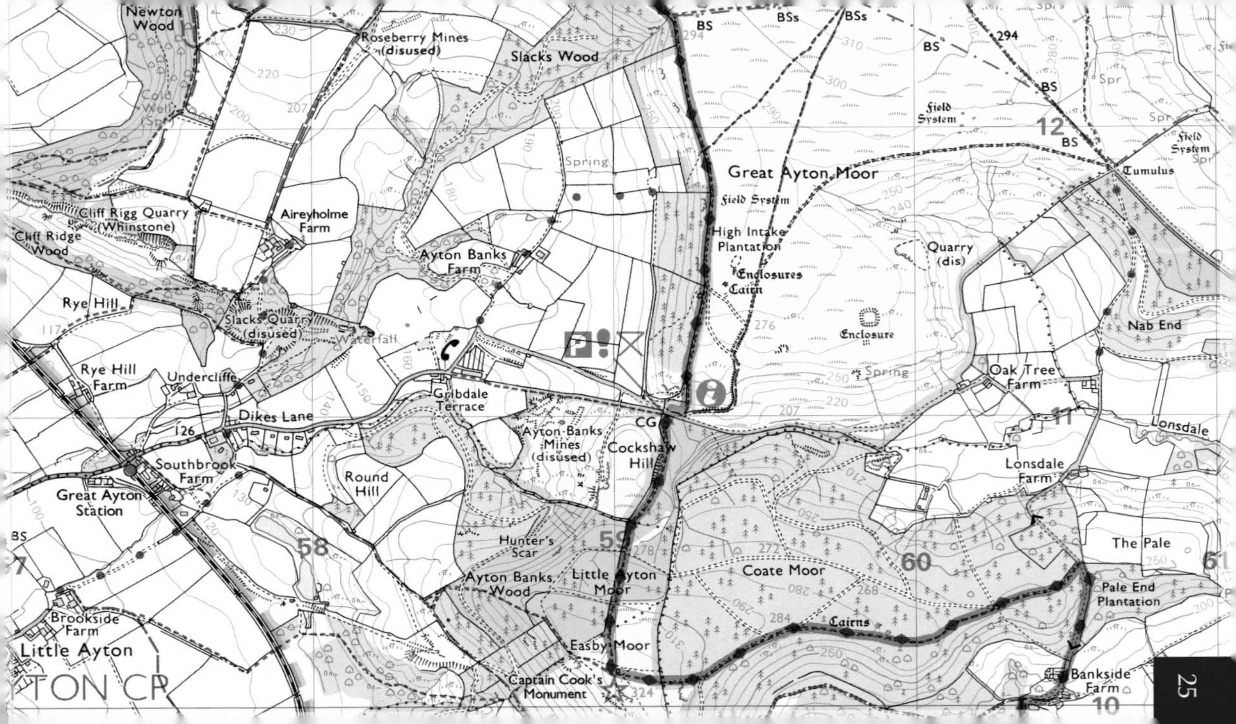
Newton Wood
Cold Well (Spr)
Roseberry Mines (disused)
Slacks Wood
Great Ayton Moor
Field System
High Intake Plantation
Enclosures
Cairn
Enclosure
Spring
Quarry (dis)
Tumulus
Nab End
Cliff Rigg Quarry (Whinstone)
Cliff Ridge Wood
Aireyholme Farm
Ayton Banks Farm
Rye Hill
Slacks Quarry (disused)
Waterfall
Rye Hill Farm
Undercliffe
Gribdale Terrace
Dikes Lane
Oak Tree Farm
Lonsdale
CG
Ayton Banks Mines (disused)
Cockshaw Hill
Southbrook Farm
Round Hill
Lonsdale Farm
Great Ayton Station
Hunter's Scar
The Pale
Ayton Banks Wood
Little Ayton Moor
Coate Moor
Pale End Plantation
Cairns
Brookside Farm
Little Ayton
Easby Moor
Captain Cook's Monument
Bankside Farm
TON CP
BS
BSs
294
324
58
59
60
61
10
11
12

The Duck
Peregrine Plantation
School
Mucky Lane (Track)
Waterfall Gill
Waterfall Wood
Sch
Horse Parks Wood
Waterfall Farm
Colleges
Hospl
Gisborough Hall
Whitby Lane
Gisborough Priory (remains of)
MP
PO
Little Waterfall Farm
Cleveland Street
GUISBOROUGH
168
Butt Lane
Foxdale Farm
Dismtd Rly
Belmont Farm
Old Park Farm
Brown Hill
Cow Pasture Hill
Schs
West Banks
Belman Bank
Shaft (dis)
Quarry (dis)
Guisborough Woods
126
Spring Wood
Shaft (dis)
Spr
Highcliff Wood
Highcliff Nab
Cairn
324
Cairn
319
Highcliff Gate Spring
Cairn
Grouse Butts
Grouse Butts (disused)
Cairn
Three Howes
Grouse Butts
284
Bethal Sla

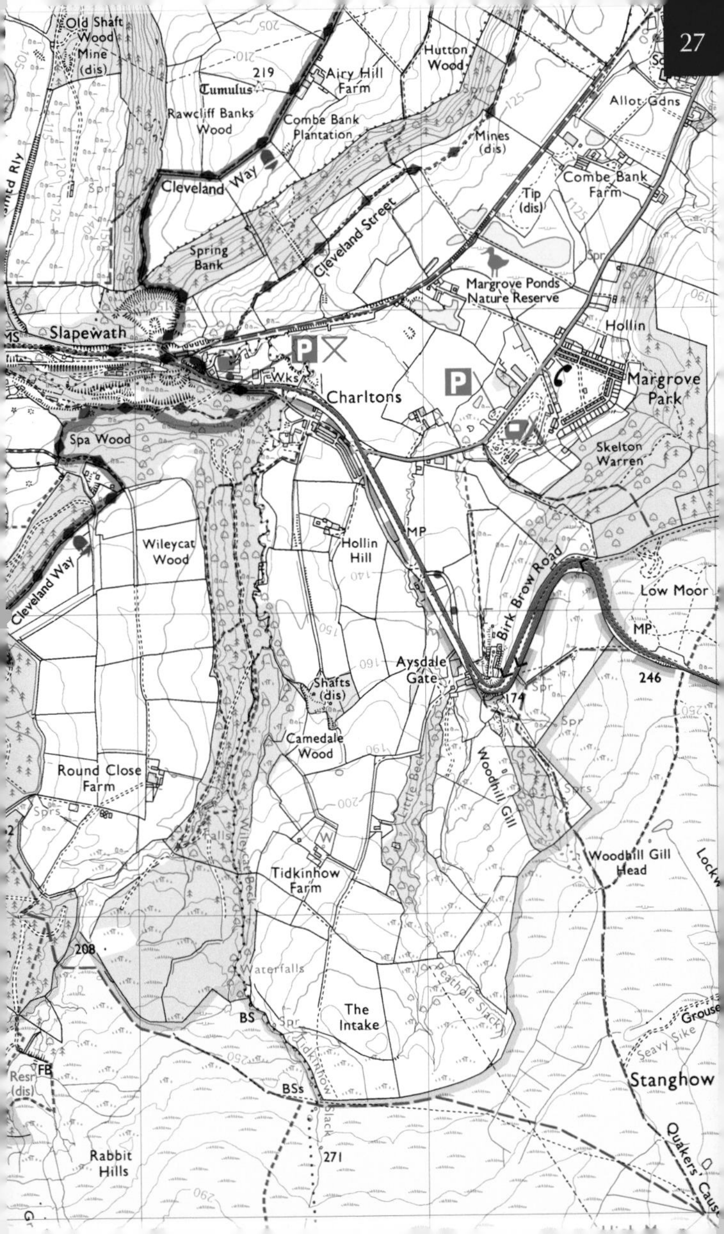

Old Shaft Wood
Mine (dis)
219
Tumulus
Airy Hill Farm
Hutton Wood
Rawcliff Banks Wood
Combe Bank Plantation
Mines (dis)
Allot Gdns
Cleveland Way
Combe Bank Farm
Tip (dis)
Cleveland Street
Spring Bank
Margrove Ponds Nature Reserve
Hollin
Slapewath
Wks
Charltons
Margrove Park
Spa Wood
Skelton Warren
Wileycat Wood
Hollin Hill
MP
Cleveland Way
Birk Brow Road
Low Moor
Aysdale Gate
Shafts (dis)
174
246
Camedale Wood
Woodhill Gill
Little Beck
Round Close Farm
Sprs
Falls
Wileycat Beck
Tidkinhow Farm
Woodhill Gill Head
208
Waterfalls
BS
The Intake
Deathole Slack
Grouse
Seavy Sike
FB
Resr (dis)
BSs
Tidkinhow Slack
Stanghow
Rabbit Hills
271
Quakers Cause

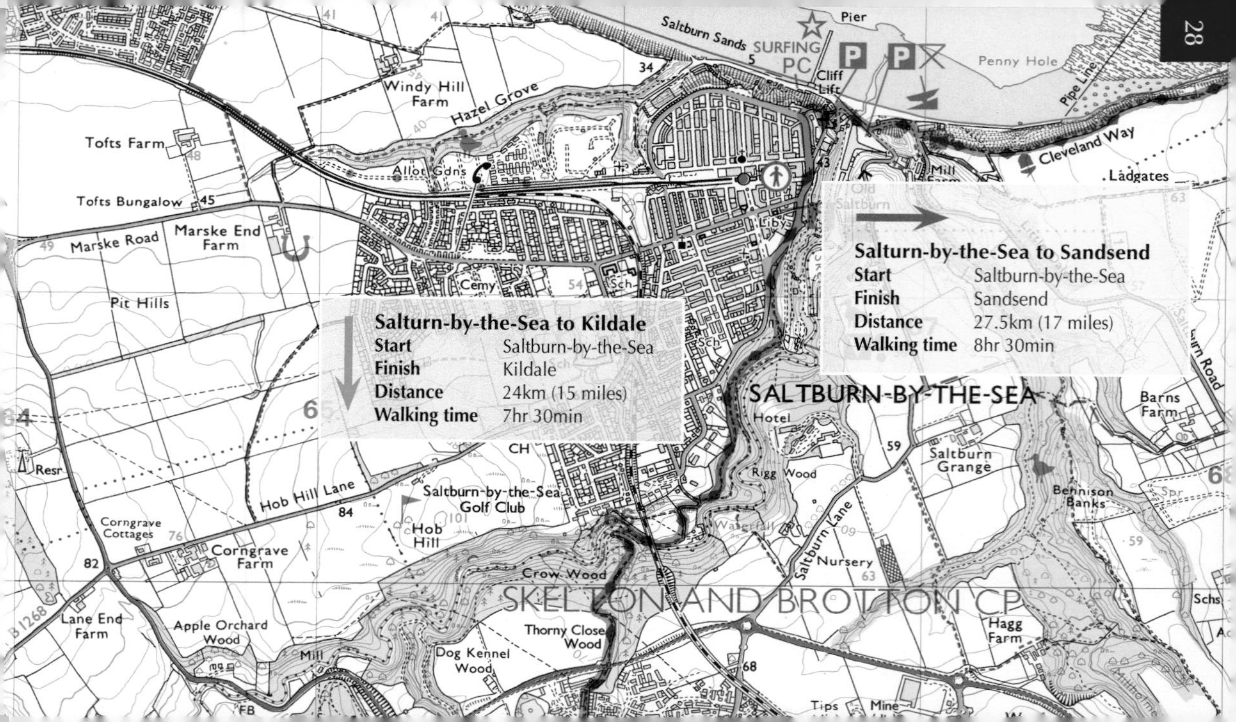
Salturn-by-the-Sea to Sandsend
Start Saltburn-by-the-Sea
Finish Sandsend
Distance 27.5km (17 miles)
Walking time 8hr 30min
Salturn-by-the-Sea to Kildale
Start Saltburn-by-the-Sea
Finish Kildale
Distance 24km (15 miles)
Walking time 7hr 30min
SALTBURN-BY-THE-SEA
SKELTON AND BROTTON CP
Saltburn Sands
Pier
SURFING
PC
Cliff Lift
Penny Hole
Pipe Line
Cleveland Way
Ladgates
Mill Farm
Old Saltburn
Saltburn Road
Barns Farm
Windy Hill Farm
Hazel Grove
Tofts Farm
Tofts Bungalow
Allot Gdns
Marske Road
Marske End Farm
Pit Hills
Cemy
Sch
Liby
Hotel
CH
Saltburn Grange
Bennison Banks
Rigg Wood
Waterfall
Saltburn Lane
Nursery
Hob Hill Lane
Saltburn-by-the-Sea Golf Club
Hob Hill
Resr
Corngrave Cottages
Corngrave Farm
Crow Wood
Lane End Farm
Apple Orchard Wood
Mill
Thorny Close Wood
Dog Kennel Wood
Hagg Farm
Schs
Tips
Mine
FB
B 1268

Millholme Farm
North Skelton
East Pastures
Industrial Estate
Layland Beck
PO
Dismantled Rly
Claphow Reservoir
Claphow Whin
Stanghow R
129
Wygrave
Holme Beck
FB
Wet Furrows Farm
98
New Skelton
White Cross Beck
Schools
Gallops
Trout Hall
Cemy
103
SKELTON
Trout Hall Lane
Priestcrofts
Boosbeck
Cold Keld (Spring)
Spr
The Hills
PO
Skelton Green
Saw Mill
Boosbeck Road
Boosbeck Bridge
Boosbeck
Manless Green Farm
Airy Hill Lane
Moat
Skelton Castle
Lawns Gill
Back Lane Farm
Cripple Hill
Marleys Wood
Spring Bank Wood
Bowman Hill
MS
88
Barns Farm
Duck Hill
Mine (dis)
High Park Plantation
Green Plantation
Park House
Skelton High Park
Lamb Hagg
Fanny Bank
FB
Skelton Beck
77

Huntcliff Foot
Bird Flight Goit
Seal Goit
Hunt Cliff
Huntcliff Cottages
Green Turf
Warsett Hill
Brough House Farm
Shepherd's House
New Brotton
Hotel
Hunley Hall Farm
Hunley Golf Club
Low Farm
Gripps Farm
Quarry (dis)
Cemy
Sch
Liby
Academy
PO
Hospital
A174
BROTTON
Resr
Carlin How
Craggs Hall
Clay
Old Tom Foot

21
Blue Nook
71
Cliff
Jetty
Cattersty Sands
Cleveland Way
72
New Gut
Resrs
Hummersea Cliff
Hummersea Scar
20
Hummersea Point
Works
Warsett Hill
121
62
Hummersea Bank
PO
Hummersea Farm
Skinningrove Farm
Skinningrove
117
Dismtd Rly
Hummersea Lane
Shaft (dis)
Spring House Farm
70
90
100
Deepdale Farm
140
Cleveland Street
PO
Sch
North Terrace
Downdinner Hill
Deepdale

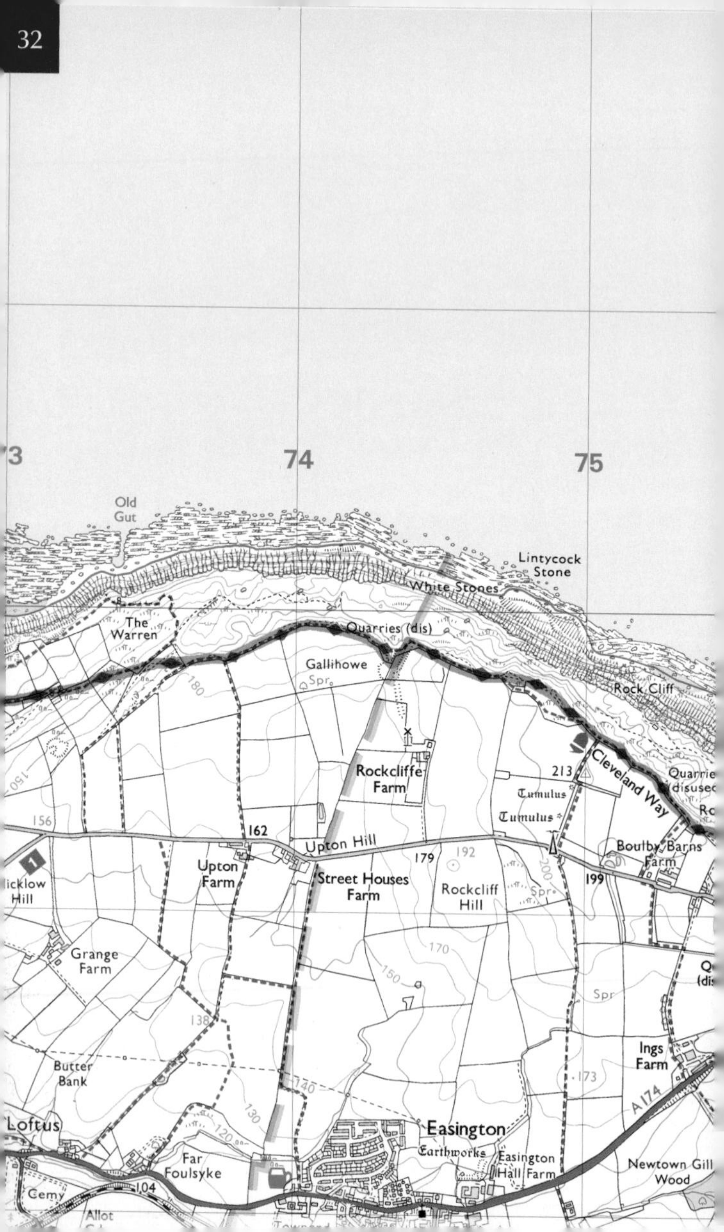
73
74
75
Old Gut
Lintycock Stone
White Stones
The Warren
Quarries (dis)
Gallihowe
Spr
180
Rock Cliff
150
Rockcliffe Farm
213
Cleveland Way
Quarries (disused)
Tumulus
Tumulus
156
162
Upton Hill
192
179
200
Boulby Barns Farm
199
Upton Farm
Street Houses Farm
Rockcliff Hill
Spr
Grange Farm
170
150
Spr
138
Ings Farm
Butter Bank
140
173
130
A174
Loftus
120
Easington
Earthworks
Easington Hall Farm
Newtown Gill Wood
Far Foulsyke
104
Allot

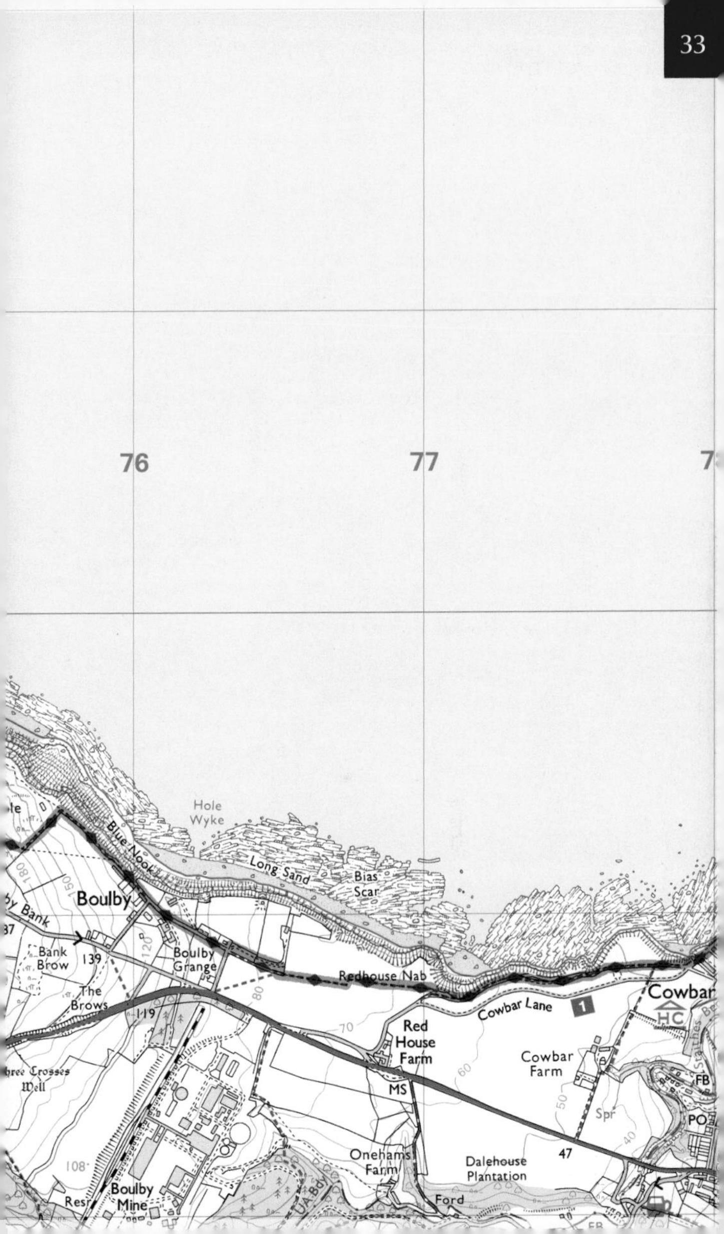
76
77
Hole
Wyke
Blue Nook
Long Sand
Bias
Scar
Boulby
Boulby Bank
Bank
Brow
139
Boulby
Grange
The
Brows
119
Redhouse Nab
Cowbar Lane
Cowbar
Red
House
Farm
Cowbar
Farm
Three Crosses
Well
MS
FB
PO
Spr
Onehams
Farm
Dalehouse
Plantation
47
Boulby
Mine
Resr
Ford
108

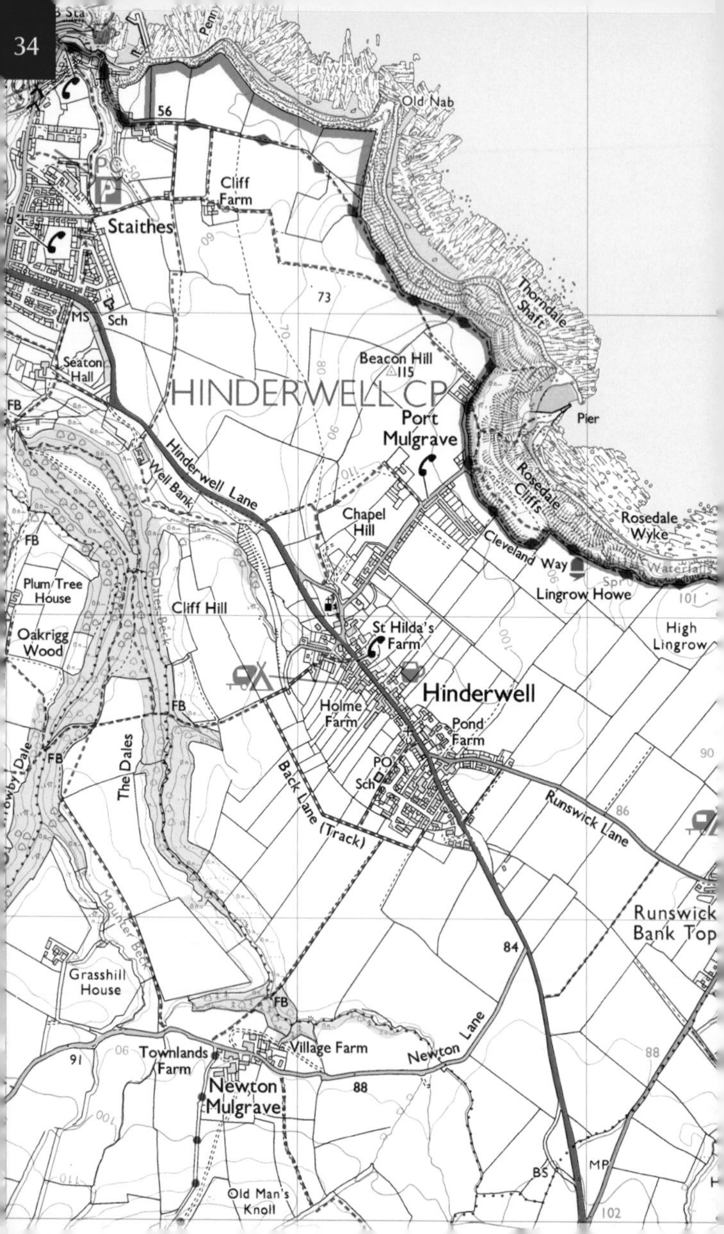
Staithes
Cliff Farm
Old Nab
Jet Wyke
56
73
Sch
MS
Seaton Hall
HINDERWELL CP
Beacon Hill
115
Thorndale Shaft
Port Mulgrave
Pier
Rosedale Cliffs
Rosedale Wyke
Cleveland Way
Lingrow Howe
Waterfalls
High Lingrow
Hinderwell Lane
Well Bank
Chapel Hill
Plum Tree House
Oakrigg Wood
Cliff Hill
Dales Beck
St Hilda's Farm
Hinderwell
Holme Farm
Pond Farm
PO
Sch
Back Lane (Track)
Runswick Lane
Runswick Bank Top
The Dales
FB
Mounter Beck
Grasshill House
84
Newton Lane
Townlands Farm
Village Farm
Newton Mulgrave
91
88
Old Man's Knoll
BS
MP
102

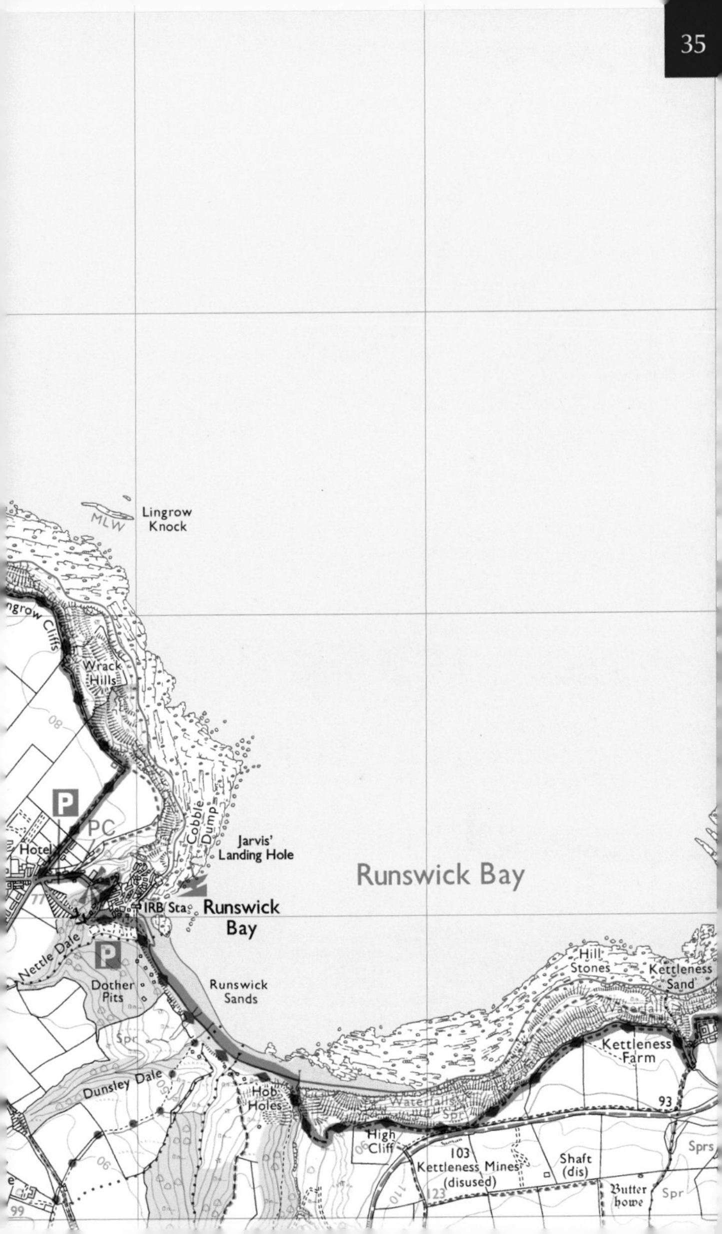
Lingrow
Knock
MLW
Lingrow Cliffs
Wrack
Hills
P
PC
Hotel
Cobble
Dump
Jarvis'
Landing Hole
Runswick Bay
IRB Sta
Runswick
Bay
Nettle Dale
P
Dother
Pits
Runswick
Sands
Spr
Dunsley Dale
Hob
Holes
Waterfalls
Spr
High
Cliff
103
Kettleness Mines
(disused)
Shaft
(dis)
Butter
howe
Spr
Sprs
93
Kettleness
Farm
Hill
Stones
Kettleness
Sand
Waterfall
123
110
99

Sandsend to Salturn-by-the-Sea

Start	Sandsend
Finish	Saltburn-by-the-Sea
Distance	27.5km (17 miles)
Walking time	8hr 30min

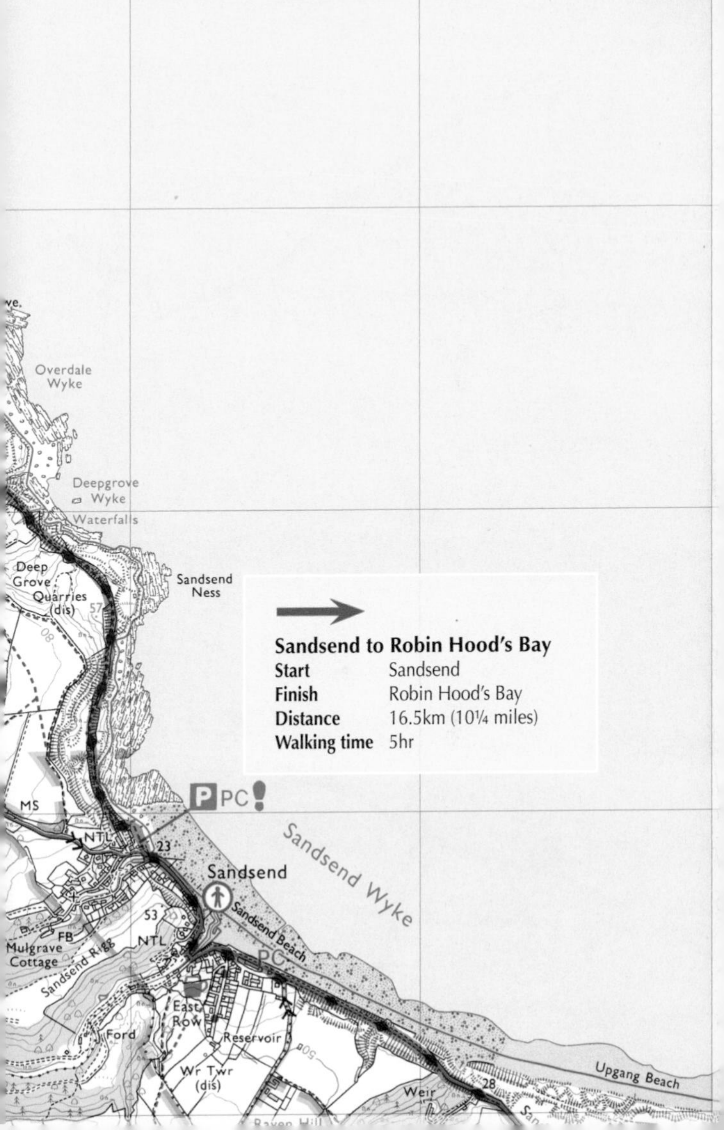

Sandsend to Robin Hood's Bay

Start	Sandsend
Finish	Robin Hood's Bay
Distance	16.5km (10¼ miles)
Walking time	5hr

Sandsend Wyke
Sandsend
Sandsend Beach
53
NTL
PC
East Row
Reservoir
Wr Twr (dis)
Raven Hill Farm
Waterfall
Home Farm
Weirs
Weir
Weirs
Waterfall
Hall
The Lake
FB
73
Raithwaite
Upgang Beach
28
Sandsend Road
Moss Brow Farm
42
Club House
FB
36
Dismtd Rly
A 174
Sandfield House
Castle Park
B 1416
High Straggleton Farm
Cliff Lane
Duck Hill
BS
Weir
Watt's Wood
Sewage Works
FB
Greystone Farm
Ewe Cote
Ewe Cote
88
Reservoirs
91
Sneaton Castle (Sch)
87
97
88
119
Newholm
Barker's Lane
102
89
BS
B1460
Garden Centre
A171
Broadings Farm
-CUM-DUNSLEY CP
Bannial Flat Farm
112
Cross Butts Farm
127
A 169
Selly Hill Farm
Guisborough Road
Works
Hawthorndale Farm
Ashes Far
Selly Hill
Aislaby Lane
BS
110
lly Cottage

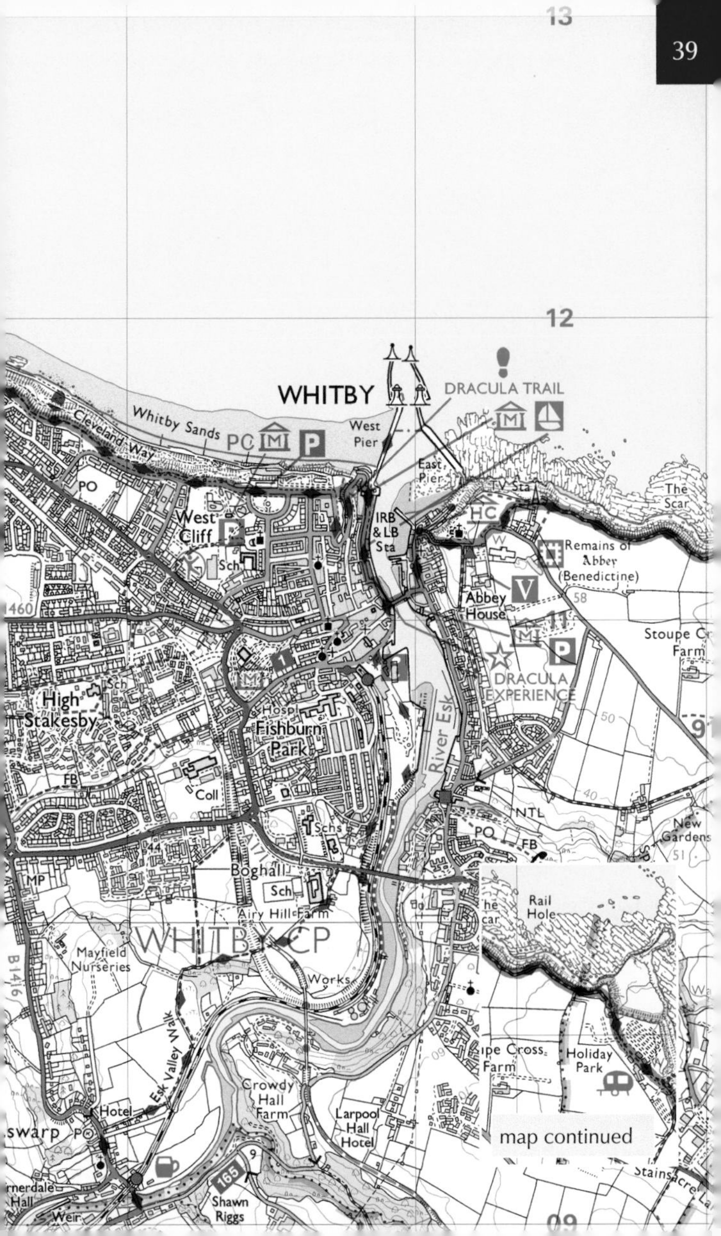

13
12
WHITBY
DRACULA TRAIL
Whitby Sands
Cleveland Way
PC
West Pier
East Pier
TV Sta
The Scar
PO
West Cliff
Sch
IRB & LB Sta
HC
Remains of Abbey (Benedictine)
58
Abbey House
11
Stoupe Cross Farm
DRACULA EXPERIENCE
460
High Stakesby
Hospl
Fishburn Park
River Esk
50
FB
Coll
NTL
40
Schs
PO
FB
New Gardens
51
44
MP
Boghall
Sch
Airy Hill Farm
WHITBY CP
Mayfield Nurseries
B1416
Works
Rail Hole
Holiday Park
Esk Valley Walk
Crowdy Hall Farm
Larpool Hall Hotel
Hotel
map continued
165
9
Shawn Riggs
Weir
09

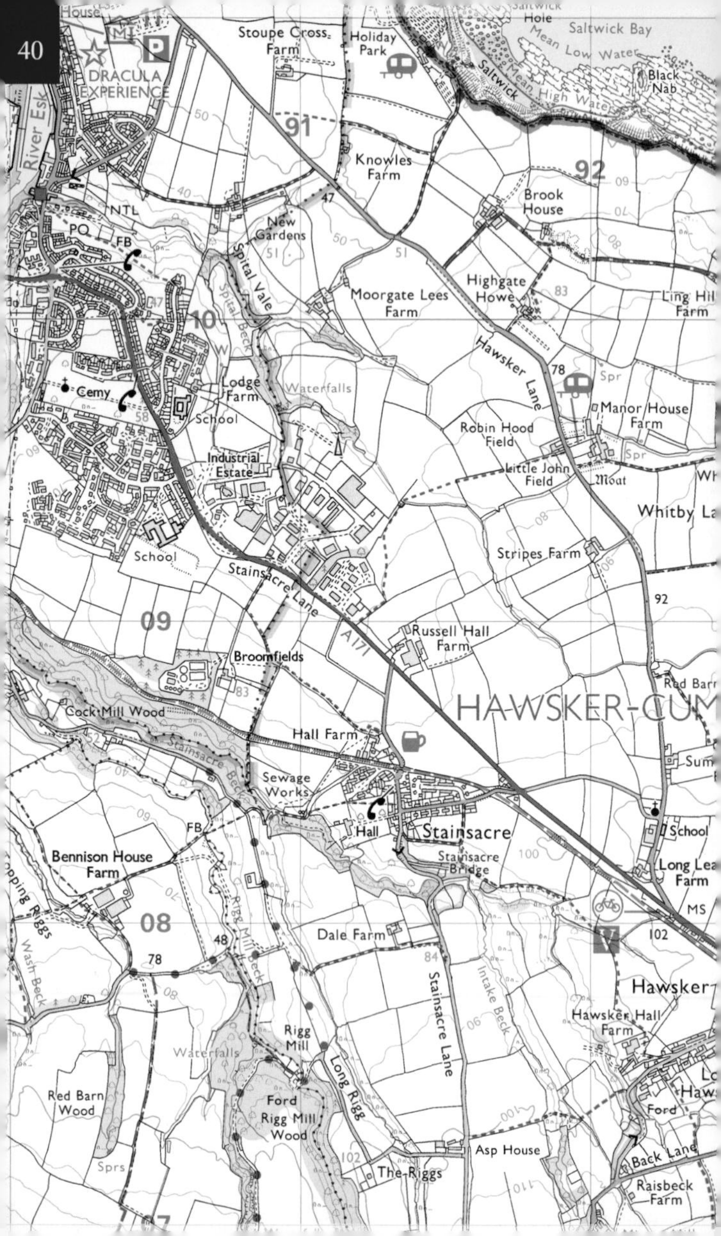

Saltwick Hole
Saltwick Bay
Mean Low Water
Black Nab
Saltwick
Mean High Water
Stoupe Cross Farm
Holiday Park
DRACULA EXPERIENCE
River Esk
91
92
Knowles Farm
Brook House
NTL
PO
FB
New Gardens
Spital Vale
Spital Beck
Moorgate Lees Farm
Highgate Howe
Ling Hill Farm
10
Hawsker Lane
Lodge Farm
Waterfalls
Cemy
School
Manor House Farm
Robin Hood Field
Industrial Estate
Little John Field
Moat
Whitby La
Stripes Farm
School
Stainsacre Lane
09
A171
Russell Hall Farm
Broomfields
Red Barn
HAWSKER-CUM
Cock Mill Wood
Hall Farm
Stainsacre Beck
Sewage Works
Hall
Stainsacre
Stainsacre Bridge
School
Long Lea Farm
Bennison House Farm
Hopping Riggs
Wash Beck
08
MS
Rigg Mill Beck
Dale Farm
Stainsacre Lane
Intake Beck
Hawsker
Hawsker Hall Farm
Rigg Mill
Waterfalls
Long Rigg
Red Barn Wood
Ford
Ford Rigg Mill Wood
Asp House
Back Lane
Sprs
The Riggs
Raisbeck Farm

93
94
Whitestone Point
97
Ling Hill
High Whitby
Pit (dis)
Widdy Head
Widdy Field
Cleveland Way
STAINSACRE CP
109
Gnipe Howe
Maw Wyke Hole
Pursglove Stye Batts
FB
Oakham Wood
Oakham Beck
Pursglove Stye
Waterfalls
Hawsker Bottoms
Northcliffe Holiday Park
108
Limekiln Slack
Ford
Spr
White Horse
High Hawsker
Reservoir
Seaview
127
B 1447
Hilda's Howe
East Close Beck
Raw Pasture Beck
Pits (dis)
Bottom House
143

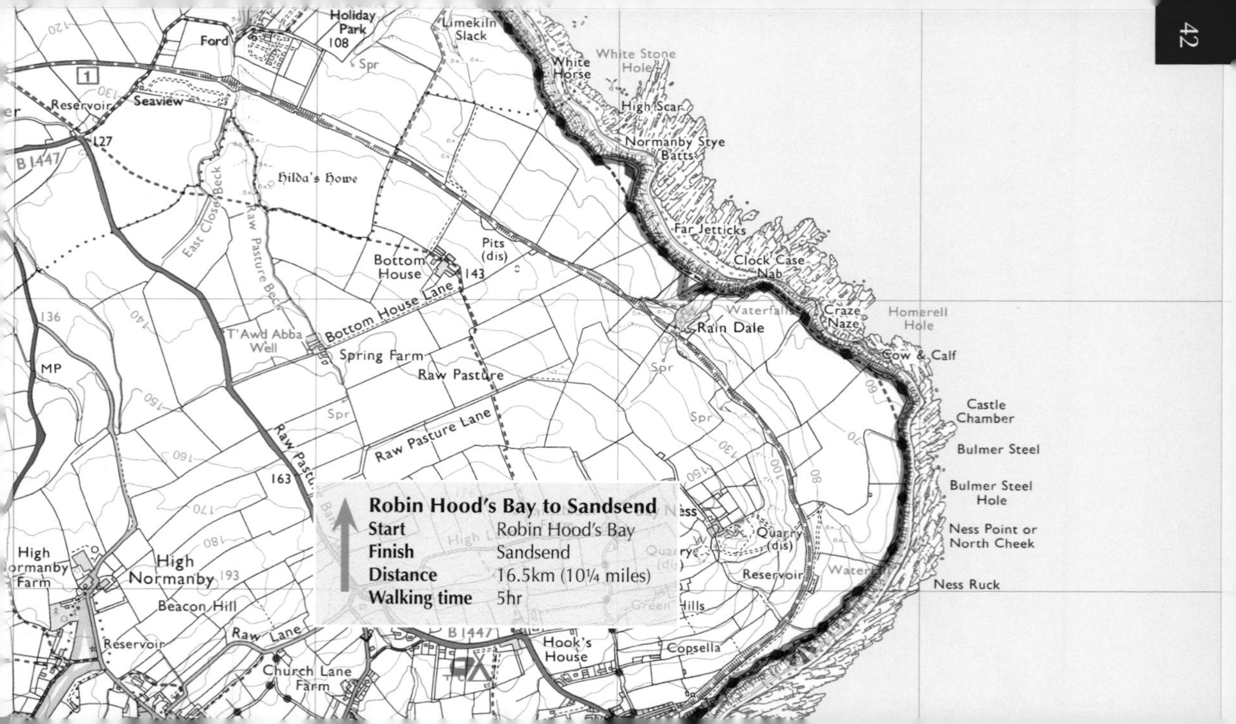
Robin Hood's Bay to Sandsend
Start Robin Hood's Bay
Finish Sandsend
Distance 16.5km (10¼ miles)
Walking time 5hr
Holiday Park
108
Limekiln Slack
Ford
White Horse
White Stone Hole
High Scar
Normanby Stye Batts
Reservoir
Seaview
127
B1447
Hilda's Howe
East Close Beck
Raw Pasture Beck
Far Jetticks
Clock Case Nab
Pits (dis)
Bottom House
143
Bottom House Lane
T'Awd Abba Well
Spring Farm
Raw Pasture
Raw Pasture Lane
Raw Pastu
163
Waterfall
Rain Dale
Craze Naze
Homerell Hole
Cow & Calf
Castle Chamber
Bulmer Steel
Bulmer Steel Hole
Ness Point or North Cheek
Ness Ruck
Quarry (dis)
Reservoir
MP
136
High Normanby Farm
High Normanby
193
Beacon Hill
Raw Lane
Church Lane Farm
Hook's House
Copsella

Robin Hood's Bay to Scarborough
Start Robin Hood's Bay
Finish Scarborough
Distance 22km (13¾ miles)
Walking time 6hr 30min
Robin Hood's Bay
Hotel
Ground Wyke
West Scar
Ground Wyke Hole
Landing Scar
East Scar
Dab Dumps
Cowling Scar
Fisher Head
Cowfield Hill
Robin Hood's Bay
Quarry Hill
FB
Hall
Sledgate Farm
Top
Fylingthorpe
Park Gate
Middlewood Farm
Yaddow Mills
Thornfields Farm
Farsyde House
Middlewood Lane
Mark Lane
High Park Wood
Fyling Hall (School)
52
56
Lodge
The Nab
Boggle Hole
Weir
FB
9
Low Farm
West Lodge
Mill Beck Farm
High Scar
Low Scar
Weir
Mill Beck
44
Ford
FB
White House
South House Farm
Tinkler's Stone
Ramsdale Beck
Wood
78
FB
Stoupe Beck Sands
Fyling Park
Gilson House
Butcher Close Wood
58
Stoupe Bank Farm
Low Balk
41
INGDALES CP
Demesne Farm
Fylingholm
Flat Scars
Bridge Holm Lane
Pit (dis)
Stoupebrow Cottage Farm
Peter White

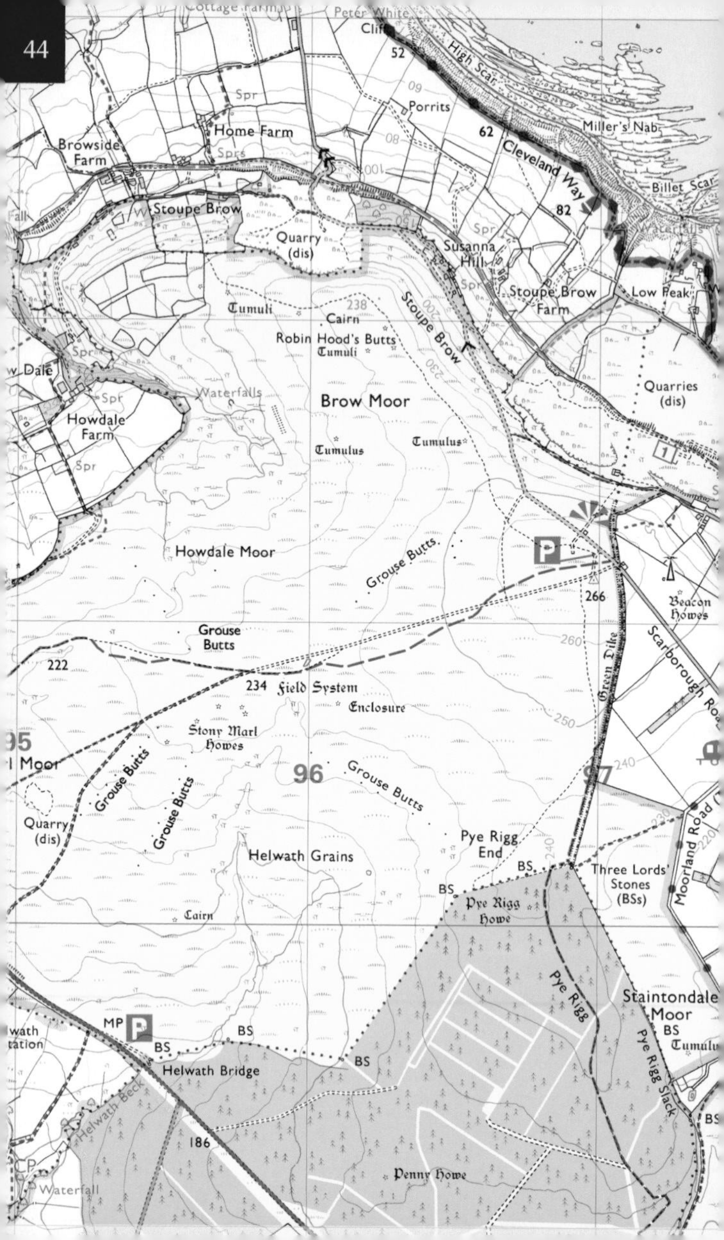

Peter White
Cliff
High Scar
Porrits
Home Farm
Browside Farm
Miller's Nab
Cleveland Way
Billet Scar
Stoupe Brow
Quarry (dis)
Susanna Hill
Stoupe Brow Farm
Low Peak
Tumuli
Cairn
Robin Hood's Butts
Stoupe Brow
Waterfalls
Brow Moor
Quarries (dis)
Howdale Farm
Tumulus
Howdale Moor
Grouse Butts
Beacon Howes
Scarborough Road
Green Dike
Field System
Enclosure
Stony Marl Howes
Quarry (dis)
Helwath Grains
Pye Rigg End
Three Lords' Stones (BSs)
Moorland Road
Pye Rigg Howe
Cairn
Pye Rigg
Staintondale Moor
Pye Rigg Slack
Helwath Bridge
Helwath Beck
Penny Howe
Waterfall

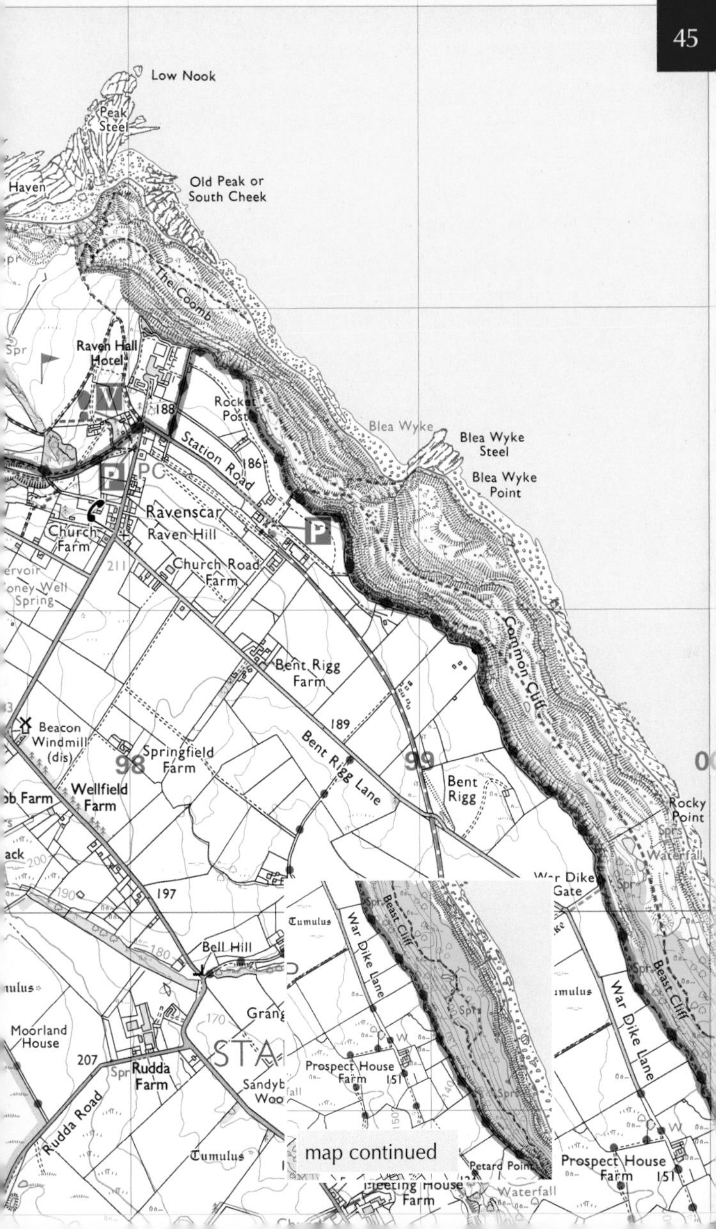
Low Nook
Peak Steel
Haven
Old Peak or South Cheek
The Coomb
Spr
Raven Hall Hotel
188
Rocket Post
Blea Wyke
Blea Wyke Steel
Blea Wyke Point
Station Road
186
PC
Ravenscar
Raven Hill
Church Farm
211
Church Road Farm
Common Cliff
Bent Rigg Farm
189
Bent Rigg Lane
Beacon Windmill (dis)
98
Springfield Farm
99
Bent Rigg
Rocky Point
Wellfield Farm
Sprs
Waterfall
200
War Dike Gate
190
197
Bell Hill
180
Tumulus
Beast Cliff
War Dike Lane
Moorland House
170
Grang
STA
207
Spr
Rudda Farm
Prospect House Farm
151
Sandyb Woo
Rudda Road
140
150
Tumulus
map continued
Petard Point
Meeting House Farm
Waterfall
00

Petard Point
124
Rigg Hall Farm
East Side Farm
109
Cleveland Way
Plane Tree Cottages
98
72
Whitehouse Farm
Herbert Hole
Whitestone
Red House Farm
Mean High Water
Mean Low Water
Hayburn Beck
Nab End
108
FB
FB
Hayburn Wyke
97
Moor Lodge
Hotel
Tindall Point
Little Cliff
99

Iron Scar
The Hulleys
Caywood Plantation
Newlands Farm
Rodger Trod
96
CLOUGHTON CP
Cloughton Newlands
Greystone Farm
Holm Slack
MS
Sycarham Farm
82
Spr
112
Little Moor
Salt Pans
Cloughton Wyke
Ripley's Bank
A171
97
Little Moor Slack
Cober
95
55
Hundale Scar
Cober Hill
Hundale Point
66
Hun Dale
Cleveland Way
Cloughton
Goose Dale
Town Farm
FBs
The Hundales
Ford
PO
Cloughton Fields Farm
Quarry Banks
Creek Point
Long Nab

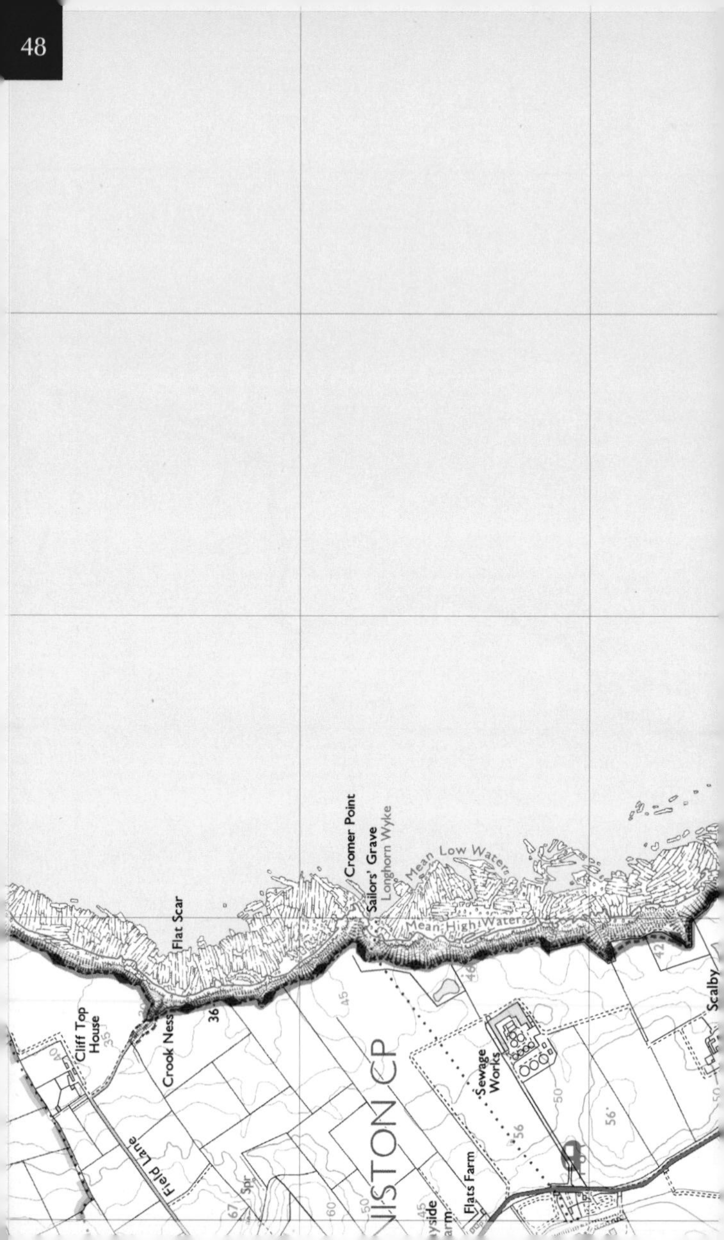
Cromer Point
Sailors' Grave
Longhorn Wyke
Mean Low Water
Mean High Water
Flat Scar
Cliff Top
House
Crook Ness
Field Lane
Sewage
Works
Flats Farm
Scalby
Spr
36
45
46
42
50
56
35
40
60
67

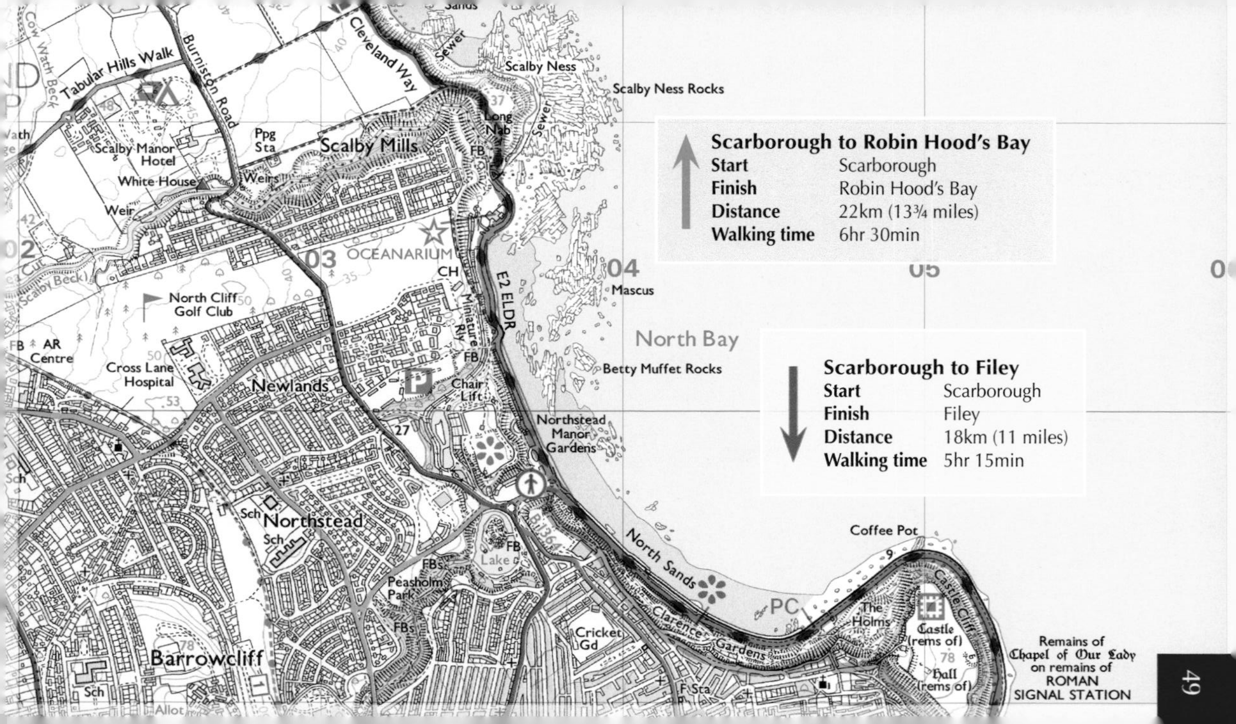
Scarborough to Robin Hood's Bay
Start Scarborough
Finish Robin Hood's Bay
Distance 22km (13¾ miles)
Walking time 6hr 30min
Scarborough to Filey
Start Scarborough
Finish Filey
Distance 18km (11 miles)
Walking time 5hr 15min
Tabular Hills Walk
Burniston Road
Cleveland Way
Scalby Ness
Scalby Ness Rocks
Long Nab
Scalby Mills
Scalby Manor Hotel
White House
Weirs
Weir
OCEANARIUM
E2 ELDR
Mascus
North Bay
Betty Muffet Rocks
North Cliff Golf Club
Cross Lane Hospital
Newlands
Miniature Rly
Chair Lift
Northstead Manor Gardens
Northstead
Peasholm Park
Lake
North Sands
Clarence Gardens
Cricket Gd
Coffee Pot
The Holms
Castle Cliff
Castle (rems of)
Hall (rems of)
Remains of Chapel of Our Lady on remains of ROMAN SIGNAL STATION
Barrowcliff
AR Centre
Cow Wath Beck
Scalby Beck
Ppg Sta
B1364

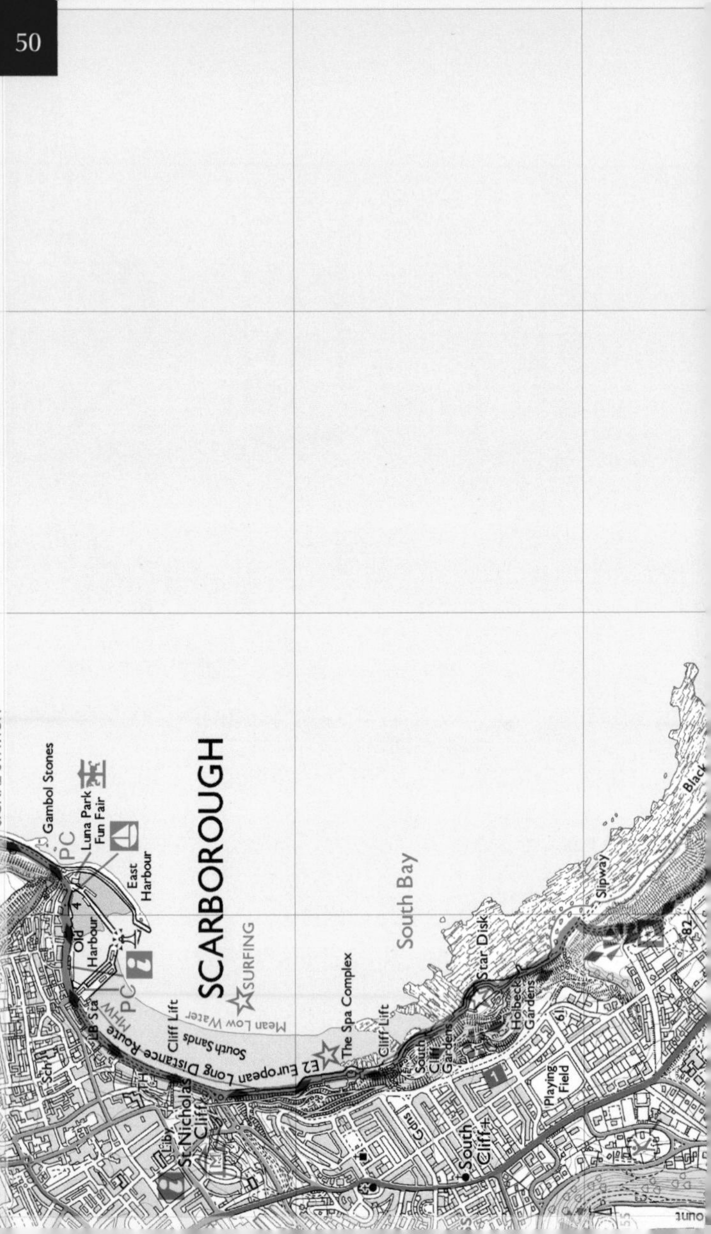

SIGNAL STATION
Gambol Stones
PC
Sch
Old Harbour
4
Luna Park Fun Fair
LB Sta
MHW
PC
East Harbour
TH
Liby
St Nicholas Cliff
Cliff Lift
E2 European Long Distance Route
South Sands
Mean Low Water
SCARBOROUGH
SURFING
The Spa Complex
Cliff Lift
South Bay
Gdns
South Cliff Gardens
South Cliff
Star Disk
Holbeck Gardens
Playing Field
61
Slipway
55
82
Black

Wheatcroft
CH
University
Scarborough South Cliff Golf Club
Pipe Line
Perilous Rocks
Outer Lake
Cornelian Bay
Inner Lake
High Scar
Ppg Sta
Frank Cliff
Cleveland Way
Knox Hill
113
74
Osgodby Point or Knipe Point
Middle Deepdale
Resr
Kit Rigg
Cayton Cliff
Johnny Flinton's Harbour
Osgodby
FB
OSGODBY CP
Deep Dale
Chapel (rems of)
78
Karl Stones
Cayton Bay
Tenants' Cliff
EASTFIELD CP
Osgodby Hill
SURFING
Calf Allen Rocks
Ppg Sta
Cayton Sands
Eastfield
Schools
Mean Low Water
Mean High Water
Red Cliff Hole
Spr
48
PC
Osgodby Lane
Playing Fields
Cow Leys Farm
Playing

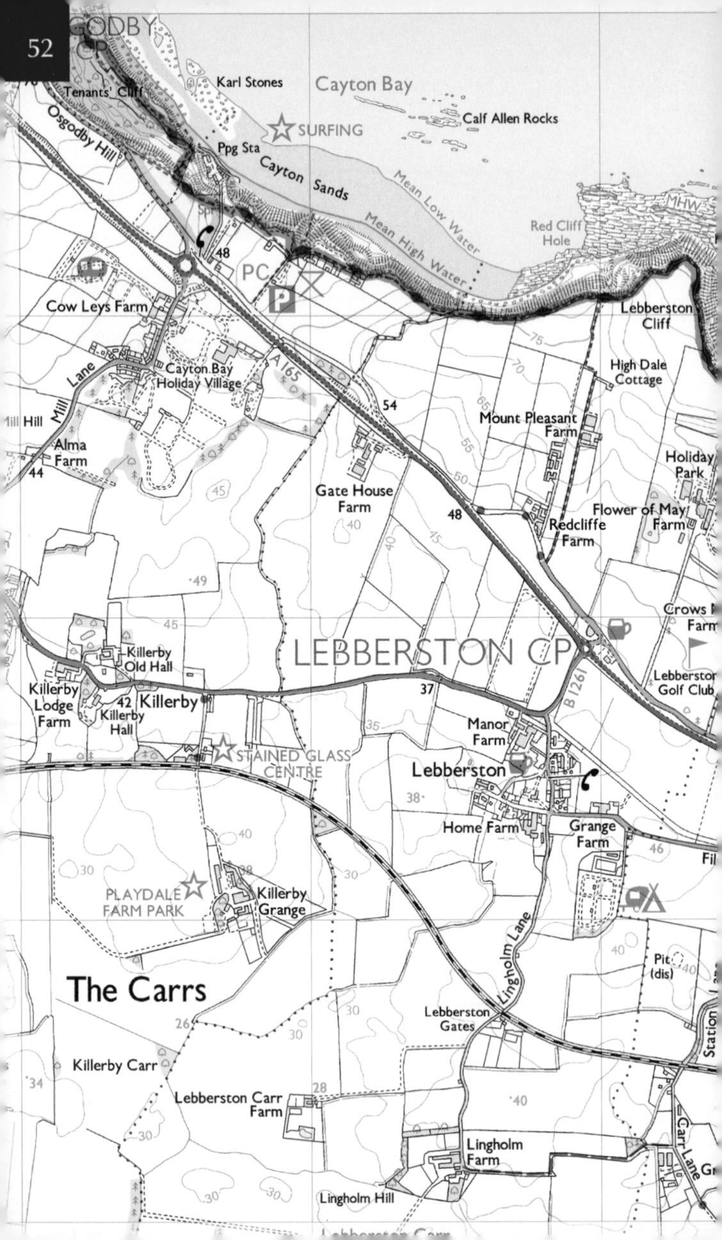
Karl Stones
Cayton Bay
Tenants' Cliff
Calf Allen Rocks
Osgodby Hill
SURFING
Ppg Sta
Cayton Sands
Mean Low Water
Mean High Water
Red Cliff Hole
MHW
48
PC
Cow Leys Farm
Lebberston Cliff
High Dale Cottage
Mill Lane
Cayton Bay Holiday Village
A165
54
Mount Pleasant Farm
Mill Hill
Alma Farm
44
Holiday Park
Gate House Farm
48
Flower of May Farm
Redcliffe Farm
49
45
LEBBERSTON CP
Killerby Old Hall
Killerby Lodge Farm
42
Killerby
Killerby Hall
37
B1261
Lebberston Golf Club
Manor Farm
STAINED GLASS CENTRE
Lebberston
Home Farm
Grange Farm
46
PLAYDALE FARM PARK
Killerby Grange
Lingholm Lane
Pit (dis)
The Carrs
Lebberston Gates
26
Killerby Carr
34
Lebberston Carr Farm
28
Lingholm Farm
Lingholm Hill
Carr Lane
Station

85
Point
ons Nab
Castle Rocks
84
Casty Rocks
Gristhorpe Sands
Old Horse Rocks
Old Horse
Gristhorpe Cliff
Great Dike
88
Blue Dolphin Holiday Park
Tumulus
90
85
Cunstone Nab
83
87
The Wyke
Cliffe House Farm
80
Cliff Farm
78
Newbiggin Cliff
Under N
75
epit Lane
GRISTHORPE CP
Cricket Gd
60
55
50
Rising Sun Farm
Hall
Newbiggin East Farm
Madge Hill
82
Filey F
Newbiggin West Farm
Moat
Carless Farm
38
40
Gristhorpe
35
A1039
30
29
Mill Hill
Filey Field Farm
Brookfield Farm
42
FB
Muston Cottage Farm
35
34
Crayke House Farm
40
e Carr
30
40
42
81

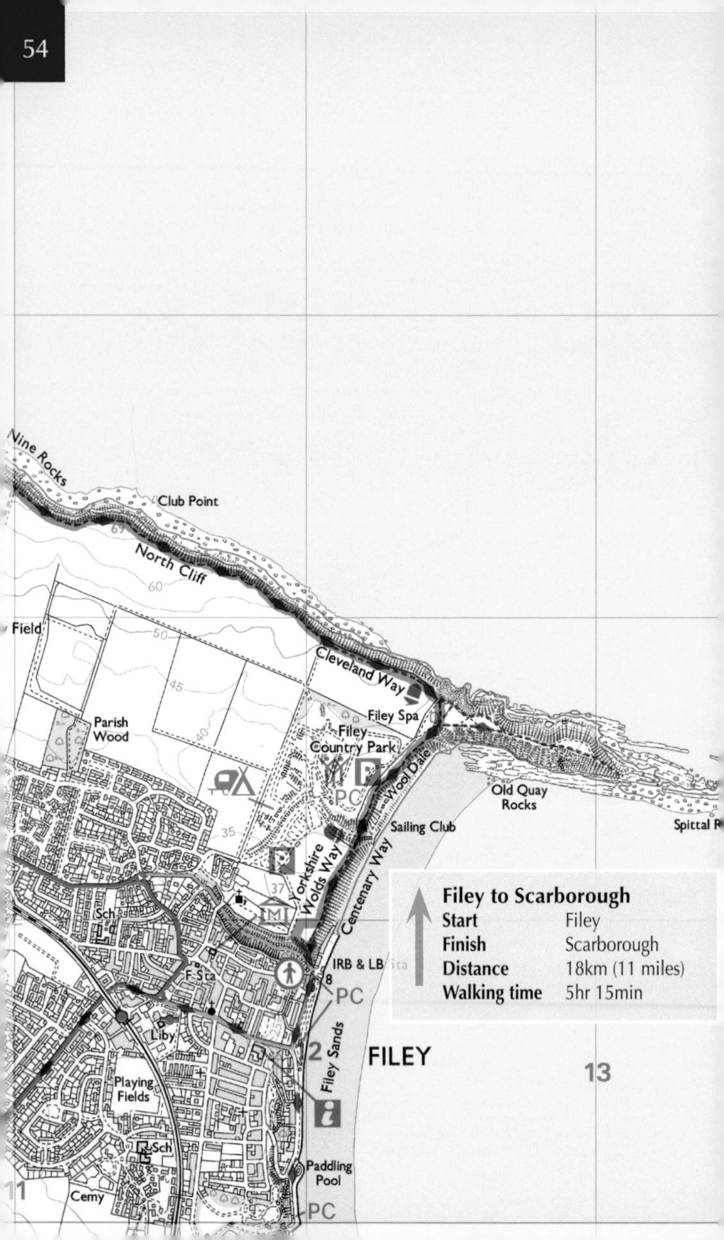

Filey to Scarborough

Start	Filey
Finish	Scarborough
Distance	18km (11 miles)
Walking time	5hr 15min

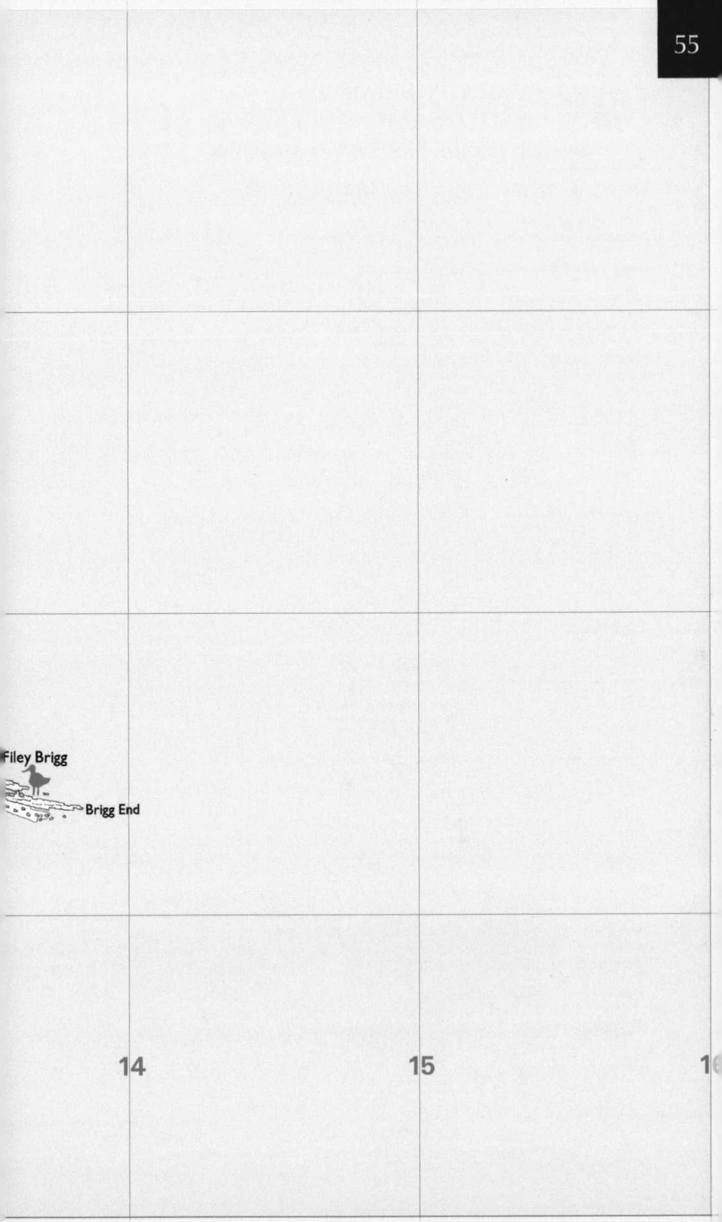

Filey Brigg

Brigg End

14

15

1

LEGEND OF SYMBOLS USED ON ORDNANCE SURVEY 1:25,000 (EXPLORER) MAPPING

ROADS AND PATHS **Not necessarily rights of way**

M1 or A6(M) Motorway — Service Area — 7 Junction Number

A 35 Dual carriageway — Service Area — T1 Toll road junction

A30 Main road

B 3074 Secondary road

Narrow road with passing places

Road under construction

Road generally more than 4 m wide

Road generally less than 4 m wide

Other road, drive or track, fenced and unfenced

Gradient: steeper than 20% (1 in 5); 14% (1 in 7) to 20% (1 in 5)

Ferry — Ferry; Ferry P – passenger only

Path

RAILWAYS

Multiple track } standard
Single track } gauge

Narrow gauge or Light rapid transit system (LRTS) and station

Road over; road under; level crossing

Cutting; tunnel; embankment

Station, open to passengers; siding

PUBLIC RIGHTS OF WAY

Footpath

Bridleway

Byway open to all traffic

Restricted byway

The representation on this map of any other road, track or path is no evidence of the existence of a right of way

ARCHAEOLOGICAL AND HISTORICAL INFORMATION

Site of antiquity — VILLA Roman — Visible earthwork

1066 Site of battle (with date) — Castle Non-Roman

Information provided by English Heritage for England and the Royal Commissions on the Ancient and Historical Monuments for Scotland and Wales

OTHER PUBLIC ACCESS

Other routes with public access — The exact nature of the rights on these routes and the existence of any restrictions may be checked with the local highway authority. Alignments are based on the best information available

Recreational route

National Trail (Long Distance Route)

Permissive footpath
Permissive bridleway
Footpaths and bridleways along which landowners have permitted public use but which are not rights of way. The agreement may be withdrawn

Traffic-free cycle route

1 1 National cycle network route number – traffic free; on road

ACCESS LAND

Firing and test ranges in the area.
Danger!
Observe warning notices

Access permitted within managed controls, for example, local byelaws. Visit **www.access.mod.uk** for information

England and Wales

Access land boundary and tint

Access land in wooded area

Access information point

Portrayal of access land on this map is intended as a guide to land which is normally available for access on foot, for example access land created under the Countryside and Rights of Way Act 2000, and land managed by the National Trust, Forestry Commission and Woodland Trust. Access for other activities may also exist. Some restrictions will apply; some land will be excluded from open access rights. The depiction of rights of access does not imply or express any warranty as to its accuracy or completeness. Observe local signs and follow the Countryside Code.
Visit **www.countrysideaccess.gov.uk** for up-to-date information

BOUNDARIES

National

County (England)

Unitary Authority (UA), Metropolitan District (Met Dist), London Borough (LB) or District
(Scotland & Wales are solely Unitary Authorities)

Civil Parish (CP) (England) or Community (C) (Wales)

National Park boundary

VEGETATION

Limits of vegetation are defined by positioning of symbols

Coniferous trees

Non-coniferous trees

Coppice

Orchard

Scrub

Bracken, heath or rough grassland

Marsh, reeds or saltings

HEIGHTS AND NATURAL FEATURES

52 · Ground survey height
284 · Air survey height

Surface heights are to the nearest metre above mean sea level. Where two heights are shown, the first height is to the base of the triangulation pillar and the second (in brackets) to the highest natural point of the hill

HEIGHTS AND NATURAL FEATURES (continued)

Vertical face/cliff

75
60
50

Loose rock | Boulders | Outcrop | Scree

Contours are at 5 or 10 metre vertical intervals

Water

Mud

Sand; sand and shingle

SELECTED TOURIST AND LEISURE INFORMATION

Building of historic interest	Nature reserve
Cadw	National Trust
Heritage centre	Other tourist feature
Camp site	Parking
Caravan site	Park and ride, all year
Camping and caravan site	Park and ride, seasonal
Castle / fort	Picnic site
Cathedral / Abbey	Preserved railway
Craft centre	Public Convenience
Country park	Public house/s
Cycle trail	Recreation / leisure / sports centre
Mountain bike trail	Roman site (Hadrian's Wall only)
Cycle hire	Slipway
English Heritage	Telephone, emergency
Fishing	Telephone, public
Forestry Commission Visitor centre	Telephone, roadside assistance
Garden / arboretum	Theme / pleasure park
Golf course or links	Viewpoint
Historic Scotland	Visitor centre
Information centre, all year	Walks / trails
Information centre, seasonal	World Heritage site / area
Horse riding	Water activites
Museum	Boat trips
National Park Visitor Centre (park logo) e.g. Yorkshire Dales	Boat hire

(For complete legend and symbols, see any OS Explorer map).

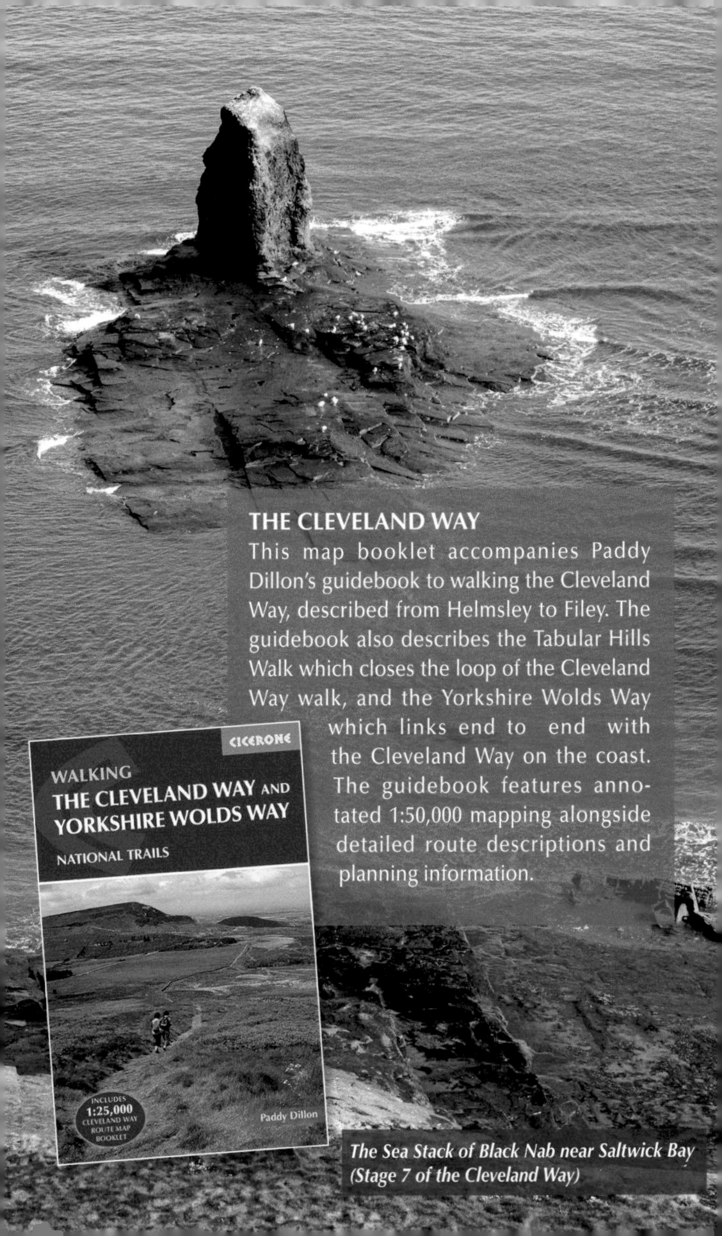

THE CLEVELAND WAY

This map booklet accompanies Paddy Dillon's guidebook to walking the Cleveland Way, described from Helmsley to Filey. The guidebook also describes the Tabular Hills Walk which closes the loop of the Cleveland Way walk, and the Yorkshire Wolds Way which links end to end with the Cleveland Way on the coast. The guidebook features annotated 1:50,000 mapping alongside detailed route descriptions and planning information.

The Sea Stack of Black Nab near Saltwick Bay (Stage 7 of the Cleveland Way)

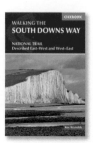

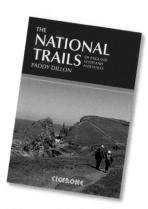

LISTING OF CICERONE GUIDES

SCOTLAND

Backpacker's Britain: Northern Scotland
Ben Nevis and Glen Coe
Cycle Touring in Northern Scotland
Cycling in the Hebrides
Great Mountain Days in Scotland
Mountain Biking in Southern and Central Scotland
Mountain Biking in West and North West Scotland
Not the West Highland Way
Scotland
Scotland's Best Small Mountains
Scotland's Mountain Ridges
The Ayrshire and Arran Coastal Paths
The Border Country
The Borders Abbeys Way
The Cape Wrath Trail
The Great Glen Way
The Great Glen Way Map Booklet
The Hebridean Way
The Hebrides
The Isle of Mull
The Isle of Skye
The Skye Trail
The Southern Upland Way
The Speyside Way
The Speyside Way Map Booklet
The West Highland Way
Walking Highland Perthshire
Walking in Scotland's Far North
Walking in the Angus Glens
Walking in the Cairngorms
Walking in the Ochils, Campsie Fells and Lomond Hills
Walking in the Pentland Hills
Walking in the Southern Uplands
Walking in Torridon
Walking Loch Lomond and the Trossachs
Walking on Arran
Walking on Harris and Lewis
Walking on Jura, Islay and Colonsay
Walking on Rum and the Small Isles
Walking on the Orkney and Shetland Isles
Walking on Uist and Barra
Walking the Corbetts Vol 1 South of the Great Glen
Walking the Corbetts Vol 2 North of the Great Glen
Walking the Galloway Hills
Walking the Munros Vol 1 – Southern, Central and Western Highlands
Walking the Munros Vol 2 – Northern Highlands and the Cairngorms
West Highland Way Map Booklet
Winter Climbs Ben Nevis and Glen Coe
Winter Climbs in the Cairngorms

NORTHERN ENGLAND TRAILS

Hadrian's Wall Path
Hadrian's Wall Path Map Booklet
Pennine Way Map Booklet
The Coast to Coast Map Booklet
The Coast to Coast Walk
The Dales Way
The Dales Way Map Booklet
The Pennine Way

LAKE DISTRICT

Cycling in the Lake District
Great Mountain Days in the Lake District
Lake District Winter Climbs
Lake District: High Level and Fell Walks
Lake District: Low Level and Lake Walks
Mountain Biking in the Lake District
Outdoor Adventures with Children – Lake District
Scrambles in the Lake District – North
Scrambles in the Lake District – South
Short Walks in Lakeland Book 2: North Lakeland
The Cumbria Way
The Southern Fells
Tour of the Lake District
Trail and Fell Running in the Lake District
Walking the Lake District Fells – Langdale
Walking the Lake District Fells – Wasdale

NORTH WEST ENGLAND AND THE ISLE OF MAN

Cycling the Pennine Bridleway
Cycling the Way of the Roses
Isle of Man Coastal Path
The Lancashire Cycleway
The Lune Valley and Howgills
The Ribble Way
Walking in Cumbria's Eden Valley
Walking in Lancashire
Walking in the Forest of Bowland and Pendle
Walking on the Isle of Man
Walking on the West Pennine Moors
Walks in Ribble Country
Walks in Silverdale and Arnside

NORTH EAST ENGLAND, YORKSHIRE DALES AND PENNINES

Cycling in the Yorkshire Dales
Great Mountain Days in the Pennines
Mountain Biking in the Yorkshire Dales
South Pennine Walks
St Oswald's Way and St Cuthbert's Way
The Cleveland Way and the Yorkshire Wolds Way
The Cleveland Way Map Booklet
The North York Moors
The Reivers Way
The Teesdale Way
Trail and Fell Running in the Yorkshire Dales
Walking in County Durham
Walking in Northumberland
Walking in the North Pennines
Walking in the Yorkshire Dales: North and East
Walking in the Yorkshire Dales: South and West
Walks in the Yorkshire Dales

WALES AND WELSH BORDERS

Cycle Touring in Wales
Cycling Lon Las Cymru
Glyndwr's Way
Great Mountain Days in Snowdonia
Hillwalking in Shropshire
Hillwalking in Wales – Vol 1
Hillwalking in Wales – Vol 2
Mountain Walking in Snowdonia
Offa's Dyke Map Booklet
Offa's Dyke Path
Pembrokeshire Coast Path Map Booklet
Ridges of Snowdonia
Scrambles in Snowdonia
Snowdonia: Low-level and easy walks – North
The Cambrian Way
The Ceredigion and Snowdonia Coast Paths
The Pembrokeshire Coast Path
The Severn Way
The Snowdonia Way
The Wales Coast Path
The Wye Valley Walk
Walking in Carmarthenshire
Walking in Pembrokeshire
Walking in the Forest of Dean
Walking in the Wye Valley
Walking on the Brecon Beacons
Walking on the Gower
Walking the Shropshire Way

DERBYSHIRE, PEAK DISTRICT AND MIDLANDS

Cycling in the Peak District
Dark Peak Walks
Scrambles in the Dark Peak
Walking in Derbyshire
White Peak Walks: The Northern Dales
White Peak Walks: The Southern Dales

SOUTHERN ENGLAND

20 Classic Sportive Rides in South East England
20 Classic Sportive Rides in South West England
Cycling in the Cotswolds
Mountain Biking on the North Downs
Mountain Biking on the South Downs
North Downs Way Map Booklet
South West Coast Path Map Booklet – Vol 1: Minehead to St Ives
South West Coast Path Map Booklet – Vol 2: St Ives to Plymouth
South West Coast Path Map Booklet – Vol 3: Plymouth to Poole
Suffolk Coast and Heath Walks
The Cotswold Way
The Cotswold Way Map Booklet
The Great Stones Way
The Kennet and Avon Canal
The Lea Valley Walk
The North Downs Way
The Peddars Way and Norfolk Coast Path
The Pilgrims' Way
The Ridgeway Map Booklet
The Ridgeway National Trail
The South Downs Way
The South Downs Way Map Booklet
The South West Coast Path
The Thames Path
The Thames Path Map Booklet
The Two Moors Way
Two Moors Way Map Booklet
Walking Hampshire's Test Way
Walking in Cornwall
Walking in Essex
Walking in Kent
Walking in London
Walking in Norfolk
Walking in Sussex
Walking in the Chilterns
Walking in the Cotswolds
Walking in the Isles of Scilly
Walking in the New Forest
Walking in the North Wessex Downs
Walking in the Thames Valley
Walking on Dartmoor
Walking on Guernsey
Walking on Jersey
Walking on the Isle of Wight
Walking the Jurassic Coast
Walks in the South Downs National Park

BRITISH ISLES CHALLENGES, COLLECTIONS AND ACTIVITIES

The Big Rounds
The Book of the Bivvy
The Book of the Bothy
The C2C Cycle Route
The End to End Cycle Route
The End to End Trail
The Mountains of England and Wales: Vol 1 Wales
The Mountains of England and Wales: Vol 2 England
The National Trails
The UK's County Tops
Three Peaks, Ten Tors

ALPS CROSS-BORDER ROUTES

100 Hut Walks in the Alps
Across the Eastern Alps: E5
Alpine Ski Mountaineering Vol 1 – Western Alps
Alpine Ski Mountaineering Vol 2 – Central and Eastern Alps
Chamonix to Zermatt
The Karnischer Hohenweg
The Tour of the Bernina
Tour of Mont Blanc
Tour of Monte Rosa
Tour of the Matterhorn
Trail Running – Chamonix and the Mont Blanc region
Trekking in the Alps
Trekking in the Silvretta and Ratikon Alps
Trekking Munich to Venice
Walking in the Alps

PYRENEES AND FRANCE/ SPAIN CROSS-BORDER ROUTES

Shorter Treks in the Pyrenees
The GR10 Trail
The GR11 Trail
The Pyrenean Haute Route
The Pyrenees
Walks and Climbs in the Pyrenees

AUSTRIA

Innsbruck Mountain Adventures
The Adlerweg
Trekking in Austria's Hohe Tauern
Trekking in the Stubai Alps
Trekking in the Zillertal Alps
Walking in Austria

SWITZERLAND

Switzerland's Jura Crest Trail
The Swiss Alpine Pass Route – Via Alpina Route 1
The Swiss Alps
Tour of the Jungfrau Region
Walking in the Bernese Oberland
Walking in the Engadine – Switzerland
Walking in the Valais

FRANCE

Chamonix Mountain Adventures
Cycle Touring in France
Cycling London to Paris
Cycling the Canal de la Garonne
Cycling the Canal du Midi
Écrins National Park
Mont Blanc Walks
Mountain Adventures in the Maurienne
The GR20 Corsica
The GR5 Trail
The GR5 Trail – Vosges and Jura
The Grand Traverse of the Massif Central
The Loire Cycle Route
The Moselle Cycle Route
The River Rhone Cycle Route
The Robert Louis Stevenson Trail
The Way of St James – Le Puy to the Pyrenees
Tour of the Oisans: The GR54
Tour of the Queyras
Vanoise Ski Touring
Via Ferratas of the French Alps
Walking in Corsica
Walking in Provence – East
Walking in Provence – West
Walking in the Auvergne
Walking in the Brianconnais
Walking in the Cevennes
Walking in the Dordogne
Walking in the Haute Savoie: North
Walking in the Haute Savoie: South
Walks in the Cathar Region

GERMANY

Hiking and Cycling in the Black Forest
The Danube Cycleway Vol 1
The Rhine Cycle Route
The Westweg
Walking in the Bavarian Alps

ICELAND AND GREENLAND

Trekking in Greenland – The Arctic Circle Trail
Walking and Trekking in Iceland

IRELAND

The Wild Atlantic Way and Western Ireland

ITALY

Italy's Sibillini National Park
Shorter Walks in the Dolomites
Ski Touring and Snowshoeing in the Dolomites
The Way of St Francis
Through the Italian Alps
Trekking in the Apennines
Trekking in the Dolomites
Via Ferratas of the Italian Dolomites Vol 1
Via Ferratas of the Italian Dolomites: Vol 2
Walking and Trekking in the Gran Paradiso
Walking in Abruzzo

Walking in Italy's Cinque Terre
Walking in Italy's Stelvio National Park
Walking in Sardinia
Walking in Sicily
Walking in the Dolomites
Walking in Tuscany
Walking in Umbria
Walking Lake Como and Maggiore
Walking Lake Garda and Iseo
Walking on the Amalfi Coast
Walks and Treks in the Maritime Alps

BELGIUM AND LUXEMBOURG

The GR5 Trail – Benelux and Lorraine
Walking in the Ardennes

SCANDINAVIA: NORWAY, SWEDEN, FINLAND

Trekking the Kungsleden
Walking in Norway

POLAND, SLOVAKIA, ROMANIA, HUNGARY AND BULGARIA

The Danube Cycleway Vol 2
The High Tatras
The Mountains of Romania
Walking in Bulgaria's National Parks
Walking in Hungary

SLOVENIA, CROATIA, SERBIA, MONTENEGRO, ALBANIA AND KOSOVO

Mountain Biking in Slovenia
The Islands of Croatia
The Julian Alps of Slovenia
The Mountains of Montenegro
The Peaks of the Balkans Trail
The Slovene Mountain Trail
Walking in Slovenia: The Karavanke
Walks and Treks in Croatia

SPAIN

Camino de Santiago – Camino Frances
Coastal Walks in Andalucia
Cycle Touring in Spain
Cycling the Camino de Santiago
Mountain Walking in Mallorca
Mountain Walking in Southern Catalunya
Spain's Sendero Historico: The GR1
The Andalucian Coast to Coast Walk
The Camino del Norte and Camino Primitivo
The Camino Ingles and Ruta do Mar
The Mountains of Nerja
The Mountains of Ronda and Grazalema
The Northern Caminos
The Sierras of Extremadura
Trekking in Mallorca
Trekking in the Canary Islands
Walking and Trekking in the Sierra Nevada
Walking in Andalucia
Walking in Menorca
Walking in the Cordillera Cantabrica
Walking on Gran Canaria
Walking on La Gomera and El Hierro
Walking on La Palma
Walking on Lanzarote and Fuerteventura
Walking on Tenerife
Walking on the Costa Blanca
Walking the Camino dos Faros

PORTUGAL

Portugal's Rota Vicentina
The Camino Portugues
Walking in Portugal
Walking in the Algarve
Walking on Madeira
Walking on the Azores

GREECE

The High Mountains of Crete
Trekking in Greece
Walking and Trekking in Zagori
Walking and Trekking on Corfu

CYPRUS

Walking in Cyprus

MALTA

Walking on Malta

INTERNATIONAL CHALLENGES, COLLECTIONS AND ACTIVITIES

Canyoning in the Alps
Europe's High Points
The Via Francigena Canterbury to Rome – Part 2

MOROCCO

Mountaineering in the Moroccan High Atlas
The High Atlas
Walks and Scrambles in the Moroccan Anti-Atlas

TANZANIA

Kilimanjaro

SOUTH AFRICA

Walking in the Drakensberg

TAJIKISTAN

Trekking in Tajikistan

JAPAN

Hiking and Trekking in the Japan Alps and Mount Fuji
Japan's Kumano Kodo Pilgrimage

JORDAN

Jordan – Walks, Treks, Caves, Climbs and Canyons
Treks and Climbs in Wadi Rum, Jordan

NEPAL

Annapurna
Everest: A Trekker's Guide
Trekking in the Himalaya

BHUTAN

Trekking in Bhutan

INDIA

Trekking in Ladakh

CHINA

The Mount Kailash Trek

NORTH AMERICA: USA AND CANADA

The John Muir Trail
The Pacific Crest Trail

SOUTH AMERICA: ARGENTINA, CHILE AND PERU

Aconcagua and the Southern Andes
Hiking and Biking Peru's Inca Trails
Torres del Paine

TECHNIQUES

Fastpacking
Geocaching in the UK
Lightweight Camping
Map and Compass
Outdoor Photography
Polar Exploration
Rock Climbing
Sport Climbing
The Mountain Hut Book

MINI GUIDES

Alpine Flowers
Avalanche!
Navigation
Pocket First Aid and Wilderness Medicine
Snow

MOUNTAIN LITERATURE

8000 metres
A Walk in the Clouds
Abode of the Gods
Fifty Years of Adventure
The Pennine Way – the Path, the People, the Journey
Unjustifiable Risk?

For full information on all our guides, books and eBooks, visit our website:
www.cicerone.co.uk